SYSTEM ARCHITECT
A Guided Tour

By
Kevin C. Dittman
and
Popkin Software & Systems Incorporated

Irwin McGraw-Hill

Boston, Massachusetts   Burr Ridge, Illinois   Dubuque, Iowa
Madison, Wisconsin   New York, New York   San Francisco, California   St. Louis, Missouri

The System Architect logo is a trademark of Popkin Software & Systems Incorporated. IBM and OS/2 are registered trademarks of IBM Corporation. Microsoft, Windows, and MS-DOS are registered trademarks of Microsoft Corporation. DBASE III plus is a trademark of Borland International.

Publication No.

Printed in the United States of America.

ISBN 0–256–19682–6

12 13 14 15 16 17 18 19 20 QPD 0 9 8

IMPORTANT - READ CAREFULLY.
By installing this software you indicate your acceptance of the following Popkin Software & Systems, Inc. Student License Agreement.

Popkin Software & Systems Inc. Student License Agreement

This is a legal agreement between you, the student, and Popkin Software & Systems Incorporated. BY INSTALLING THIS SOFTWARE, YOU ARE AGREEING TO BE BOUND BY THE TERMS OF THIS AGREEMENT. IF YOU DO NOT AGREE TO THE TERMS OF THIS AGREEMENT, PROMPTLY RETURN THE SOFTWARE PACKAGE AND THE ACCOMPANYING ITEMS (including written material and binder or other containers) TO THE PLACE YOU OBTAINED THEM FOR A FULL REFUND.

POPKIN SOFTWARE & SYSTEMS SOFTWARE LICENSE

1.   **GRANT OF LICENSE.** Popkin Software & Systems grants you the right to use the "SOFTWARE" according to the terms and conditions herein. The "SOFTWARE" is defined to be the enclosed Popkin Software & Systems software program and all subsequent updates to the software program legally received by you. This License Agreement permits a single user to install the "SOFTWARE" on only one computer at one location at any one time. You may use the Software solely for the purpose of learning software engineering and improving your skills. The Software may not be used for any commercial purpose, either for your benefit or the benefit of any other party.

2.   **TERM.** This License Agreement is effective from the day you receive the "SOFTWARE", and continues until you return the original magnetic media and all copies of the "SOFTWARE" to Popkin Software & Systems. Popkin Software & Systems shall have the right to terminate this license if you violate any of its provisions. Popkin Software & Systems is the owner of all rights from which this license emanates.

3.   **COPYRIGHT.** The "SOFTWARE" is owned by Popkin Software & Systems or its suppliers and is protected by United States copyright laws and international treaty provisions. Therefore, you must treat the "SOFTWARE" like any other copyrighted material (e.g., a book or musical recording) except that you may make a single copy of the "SOFTWARE" for archival purposes only. You may not copy the written materials accompanying the "SOFTWARE". You must reproduce and include any copyrights and trademark notices on all copies. You must maintain an accurate record of the location of all copies at all times.

4.   **OTHER RESTRICTIONS.** You may not rent or lease the "SOFTWARE", but you may transfer the "SOFTWARE" and accompanying written materials on a permanent basis provided (a) you provided Popkin Software & Systems written notice of your name (or, if applicable, the name of your business) and the name and address of the person or entity to whom you intend to transfer the rights granted by this Agreement, (b) you retain no copies and (c) the recipient agrees to the terms of this agreement. You may not reverse engineer, decompile or disassemble the "SOFTWARE", except to the extent that the foregoing restriction is expressly prohibited by applicable law. You may not alter or modify the "SOFTWARE".

NO WARRANTIES. Popkin Software & Systems expressly disclaims any warranty for the "SOFTWARE". The "SOFTWARE" and any related documentation is provided "as is" without warranty of any kind.

Popkin Software & Systems does NOT warrant that the "SOFTWARE" will meet your requirements or that the operation of the "SOFTWARE" will be uninterrupted and error free. You are solely responsible for the selection of the "SOFTWARE" to achieve your intended results and for the results actually obtained.

CUSTOMER REMEDIES. Popkin Software & Systems' entire liability and your exclusive remedy shall not exceed the price paid for the "SOFTWARE".

NO OTHER WARRANTIES. POPKIN SOFTWARE & SYSTEMS DISCLAIMS ALL OTHER WARRANTIES, EITHER EXPRESS OR IMPLIED, INCLUDING BUT NOT LIMITED TO IMPLIED WARRANTIES OF MERCHANTABILITY AND FITNESS FOR A PARTICULAR PURPOSE, WITH RESPECT TO THE "SOFTWARE", AND THE ACCOMPANYING WRITTEN MATERIALS. THIS LIMITED WARRANTY GIVES YOU SPECIFIC LEGAL RIGHTS. YOU MAY HAVE OTHERS, WHICH VARY FROM STATE TO STATE.

NO LIABILITY FOR CONSEQUENTIAL DAMAGES. IN NO EVENT SHALL POPKIN SOFTWARE & SYSTEMS OR ITS SUPPLIERS BE LIABLE FOR ANY DAMAGES WHATSOEVER (INCLUDING, WITHOUT LIMITATION, DAMAGES FOR LOSS OF BUSINESS PROFITS, BUSINESS INTERRUPTION, LOSS OF BUSINESS INFORMATION, OR OTHER PECUNIARY LOSS) ARISING OUT OF THE USE OR INABILITY TO USE THIS POPKIN SOFTWARE & SYSTEMS PRODUCT, EVEN IF POPKIN SOFTWARE & SYSTEMS HAS BEEN ADVISED OF THE POSSIBILITY OF SUCH DAMAGES AND EVEN IF THE "SOFTWARE" FAILS OF ITS ESSENTIAL PURPOSE. BECAUSE SOME STATES DO NOT ALLOW THE EXCLUSION OR LIMITATION OF LIABILITY FOR CONSEQUENTIAL OR INCIDENTAL DAMAGES, THE ABOVE LIMITATION MAY NOT APPLY TO YOU.

U.S. GOVERNMENT RESTRICTED RIGHTS

The "SOFTWARE" and documentation are provided with RESTRICTED RIGHTS. Use, duplication, or disclosure by the Government is subject to restrictions as set forth in subdivision (c)(1)(ii) of The Rights in Technical Data and Computer Software Clause at 48 C.F.R. 252.227-7013 or subparagraphs (c)(1) and (2) of the Commercial Computer Software Restricted Rights of 48 CFR 52.227-19, as applicable. Contractor/manufacturer is Popkin Software & Systems Inc./11 Park Place,/New York. NY 10007.

This agreement is governed by the laws of New York.

Should you have any questions concerning this Agreement, or if you desire to contact Popkin Software & Systems, Inc. for any reason, please write Popkin Software & Systems Inc./11 Park Place/New York, NY 10007.

5000\1\AGR0031_.DTJ

Table of Contents

Preface

Purpose and Scope

The purpose of this document is to provide you with a tutorial to be used with the Student, Laboratory and University versions of System Architect. The information provided within this manual will assist you in installing the Student version of System Architect, and to help you become familiar with the basic techniques of the software.

This manual was adapted from the *Configuration Guide, Tutorial*, and *System Architect Fundamentals,* manuals produced by Popkin Software. It will provide you with a basic understanding of how to use System Architect to draw diagrams, define data, and customize the properties (characteristics) of your diagrams, symbols, and definitions.

Audience

This document is designed for a student who has purchased the Student version of System Architect. It provides them with step by step instructions on setting up encyclopedias, creating diagrams, and producing reports. Each chapter has a set of review questions that re-emphasize the major topics of the chapter.

This document assumes you are familiar with operating in a Microsoft Windows environment, and that you are familiar with the concepts of creating system models using structured analysis techniques. There are many good text books for structured analysis and data modeling, consult with your professor or your school librarian for recommendations.

System Architect supports most of the major analysis and design methodologies.
They are listed in the Table 1. below, and sub-divided into four basic groups.

Data Modeling	Entity Relation Diagram IDEF1X Logical View Diagram SQL Physical Diagram
Structured Analysis & Design	Gane & Sarson Data Flow Diagram IDEF0 Ward & Mellor Data Flow Diagram (for real-time applications) Yourdon/DeMarco Data Flow Diagram SSADM IV State Transition Diagram State Transition Diagram, Ward & Mellor (for real-time applications) Structure Chart
Business Process Re- engineering	IDEF0 IDEF1X
Object-oriented Analysis & Design (optional)	Booch '94 Coad/Yourdon OMT/Rumbaugh Shlaer/Mellor Use Case

Table 1. Supported Methodologies

System Architect supports other diagram types, which are generally useful,
regardless of which methodology you may be using: Auto-decomposition and
Decomposition Diagrams, Flow Chart, Character Screen, Graphic Screen, and
Menu Screen[1].

---

[1] The character, graphic and menu screen diagrams are available with the SA Screen Painter option.

Document Conventions

This document adheres to the following document conventions:

- **bolding**

    Indicates the name of a System Architect menu, menu command, or dialog box command. For example:

    Click on the **Diagram** Menu.

- *italics*

    Marks the first appearance of a commonly-used term in either the System Architect or the Microsoft Windows environment. For example:

    Click on the cursor symbol in the upper left-hand corner of the *Toolbox*.

    Italics are used when reference is made to a methodology term, as in:

    All *process* symbols have names.

    Italics are also used when a cross-reference is made to another section of this manual, as in:

    More information will be found in *Section 2, Quick Start.*

- courier

    Indicates user input. For example:

    COPY A:*.* C:\SYSARCH

I. Installing System Architect

I.1 System Requirements

System Architect requires the following minimum hardware and software configuration:

- An IBM compatible PC with a 80386 or greater processor; 80486 DX 33 MHz or greater is recommended.

- A minimum of 4 MB of installed RAM.

- Version 5.0 or later of the MS-DOS operating system, and Version 3.1 or later of the Microsoft Windows graphical-interface system.

- A graphics display adapter, supported by the Microsoft Windows system. VGA or better is required.

- A mouse input device supported by the Microsoft Windows system.

- One high density 3 1/2" floppy-disk drive (for installation and backups).

- One disk drive with at least 10 MB (megabytes) of free disk space after installation of System Architect.

I.2 Installing the Student Version

☞ *WARNING: For safety, you should make backup copies of the System Architect diskettes before you use them in the System Architect installation procedure.*

☞ *A README.TXT file is included on Diskette 1 of the System Architect Program diskettes. Complete instructions for installing the System Architect software package on your system will be found in that file. Please be sure to read its contents before beginning the installation procedure. You can use any text or non-text file editor, such as Windows Notepad to display (and print) the README.TXT file.*

You have received 3 program diskettes for the Educational (Student) version of System Architect 3.0. These disks contain the executable module, the required DLL's, and a help file. Some files are compressed.

To install System Architect on your hard drive:

1. Insert Program Diskette 1 into your floppy drive (a: or b:).

2. With Windows already running, pull down the **File** menu in the Program Manager.

3. Choose the **Run** command.

4. Type A:\SETUP or B:\SETUP on the command line, then click on **OK**.

5. You will be prompted to name the directory in which System Architect is to be installed. The installation program defaults to the C:\SYSARCH directory.

6. You will be prompted to change diskettes during the installation process.

I.3 The Educational Version of System Architect

The Educational version of System Architect does not require a key device to operate. Copying this software is prohibited.

The encyclopedias created using the Educational version of System Architect are encrypted. If your school is using the University version of System Architect in their computer laboratory, we strongly recommend that you ask your professor to provide you with a replacement SAEDUCA.DLL file which will change the encryption scheme so that you may work on the same encyclopedia either in your school's computer lab, or on your home computer. **If you create an encyclopedia and subsequently replace your SAEDUCA.DLL file, you will not be able to access any of the diagrams or definitions that were created prior to changing SAEDUCA.DLL.**

Refer to *Appendix C* for the number of diagrams and definitions that can be created using the Educational Student and Lab versions of System Architect.

I.4 After Completing Installation

Now that you've completed the installation of System Architect, you're ready to start your first project. The remainder of this Manual contains sections that explain how to get a project going, how to draw symbols and define the data, processes, tables, relationships, and other objects needed for a project. Working your way through the each section should take about one hour.

1. Introduction

This section provides a brief introduction to System Architect. It answers questions that are sometimes asked by new users:

- What is System Architect?
- What diagram types and modeling techniques are supported?
- How is the system development life cycle affected by using this tool?

1.1 Introduction to System Architect

System Architect is a PC-based CASE tool that maintains relationships between every object and every other object in a system, plus automates the process of generating, manipulating, organizing, and managing the following kinds of system-modeling diagrams:

- Gane & Sarson data flow
- Ward & Mellor data flow (real time)
- Yourdon/DeMarco data flow
- Decomposition
- Entity relation
- Flow Chart
- IDEF0
- IDEF1X
- Logical View
- State transition
- Ward & Mellor state transition
- Structure chart
- SSADM IV
- Database Physical Models
- Object-oriented design: Booch, Coad-Yourdon, & OMT (optional)
- Graphical User Interface (GUI) Screens and Menus (optional)
- Character-based Screens (optional)

1.2 Systems Modeling and System Architect

1.2.1 Graphic Languages

Systems modeling is the process of describing an existing or proposed system. A model is constructed, which is used to analyze the system, and optimize its functionality. Most of the modeling techniques used for analysis and design involve graphic languages. These graphic languages are sets of symbols that, when used according to the rules of the methodology, can communicate the complex relationships of information systems more clearly than narrative text. The goal of any CASE tool is to assist you in understanding, learning, and using these graphic languages.

1.2.2 Hierarchical Organization

Any documentation, whether it uses a graphic language or a written one, must be organized and broken down into understandable pieces. In systems modeling, systems are partitioned into subsystems (a top-down approach), and related objects or data are grouped into simplified abstracted objects (a bottom-up approach), to show only the level of detail required to communicate a specific relationship.

1.2.3 The Data Dictionary

The definitions for the graphic objects on the diagram, and the data definitions, are stored in a centralized data dictionary. The data dictionary together with the symbols, connections, and diagrams are referred to as the *Encyclopedia*. The Encyclopedia is also sometimes referred to as a *Repository*.

Unlike language dictionaries, which provide volumes of linear information, a CASE data dictionary is a machine-readable database of information that can be queried, cross referenced, and updated continually. The data dictionary is integrated with the graphic objects, so that changes made in one place can be automatically reflected in other places.

1.2.4 The System Architect Strategy

System Architect is a platform for developing systems. It is a collection of tools, and a database of the information created with the tools. The tools make possible, the various diagramming techniques, program documentation, or project management analysis, essential to modern systems engineering. The

tools are based on rigorous methodologies, yet each can be customized. The tools
are integrated in System Architect with a consistent user interface, and access
the centralized database of information called the encyclopedia.

1.3 Questions In Review

1. What is System Architect?

2. Name five diagram types that System Architect supports.

3. Define Systems modeling.

4. What are graphic languages?

5. What does System Architect's encyclopedia consist of?

Answers to the above questions can be found in Appendix B.

2. Starting System Architect

1. Start System Architect by pointing inside the System Architect program icon and double-clicking on it.

2. The Audit Id dialog box comes up on top of the System Architect window. In the dialog box type a personal identifier of up to 7 characters.

Figure 2-1 Starting System Architect

3. Click on **OK** (or press Enter).

Hint System Architect automatically adds the Audit ID to all diagrams and dictionary definitions. Use it to report on work that you create or modify.[1]

The Audit Id is not a password. You may use any combination of letters and numbers you wish.

4. If this is the first time you are bringing System Architect up after installation, you will be asked if you wish to create the Path and Encyclopedia C:\SYSARCH\PROJECT1. Click on **No**. You will create the appropriate path and encyclopedia for this manual in the next section.

2.1 Creating an Encyclopedia

System Architect stores the work of each project (or sub-project) in a separate encyclopedia. An encyclopedia is made up of a set of DBASE III Plus files for storing all diagrams and dictionary definitions. The name of an encyclopedia is the same as the name of the directory under which System Architect created its DBASE files. In the student edition of System Architect you can create up two encyclopedias. In the University version you can create encyclopedias up to the limit of your available disk space.

☞   *Do not attempt to modify any System Architect files using other products. Only System Architect can modify these files without damaging them.*

Your next step is to create an encyclopedia in the sub-directory called PROJECT1.

---

[1] The reports in the Audit Trail group in REPORTS.RPT will list dictionary information added and/or modified by Audit Id and type.

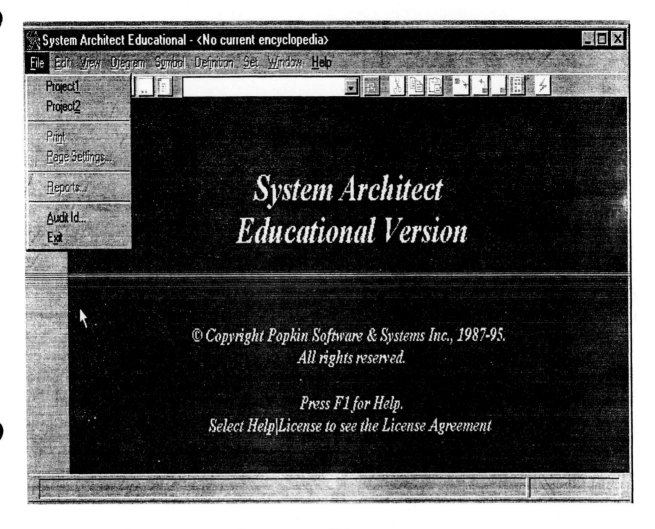

Figure 2-2. File menu

To create an encyclopedia in the PROJECT1 sub-directory:

    1. Pull down the **File** menu and select the **Project1** command.

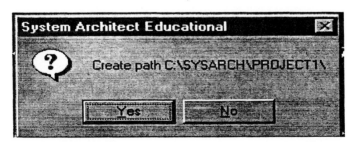

Figure 2-3. Click on **Yes** to Create a New Path

    2. Click on **Yes** in response to the question **Create Path
       C:\SYSARCH\PROJECT1\.** The next message is:

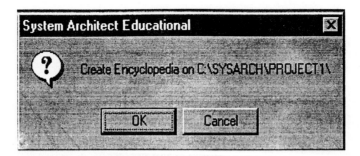

Figure 2-4. Click on **OK** to Create the Encyclopedia

3. Click on **OK** in response to the question **Create Encyclopedia on C:\SYSARCH\PROJECT1\.**

2.2 Setting Your Session Preferences

The **Preferences** dialog contains a series of check boxes. Some of these preferences affect the balance of control between having System Architect check, control and prompt your actions, and your freedom to do these functions at your own discretion. The right balance might change as you progress through different stages of diagramming. For instance, you would probably start a diagram with the preference **Auto Reposition Name** turned on, and turn it off after the rough symbol placement was completed to preserve the name placement prior to final editing of symbol positions.

To modify your preference settings:

1. Pull down the **Set** menu.

2. Click on the **Preferences** command. The **Preferences** dialog opens.

3. Toggle on or off each of the check boxes to enable or disable each feature as shown in *Figure 2-5.*

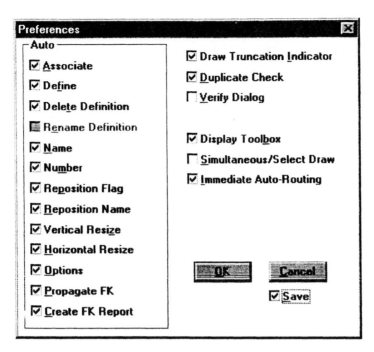

Figure 2-5. **Preferences** Dialog from the **Set** Menu

4. Click the **Save** box to change the default to the current settings.

5. Click **OK** to save the settings for the current working session and close the dialog.

The default values shown in *Figure 2-5* are appropriate for a new user; they provide some automated assistance and limited prompting.

The preference settings are applied globally to all symbol types; however, they may need to be enabled for individual symbol types. *Appendix A* contains the list of preference settings, and indicates what each preference setting applies to, where it is enabled from for specific symbol types, and its function.

2.3 Characteristics of Symbols and Labels

This section introduces the generic characteristics of graphic symbols, lines, and names.

2.3.1 Characteristics of Rectangular and Line Symbols

Rectangular symbols are predefined, enclosed shapes such as rectangles or rounded rectangles. Ward & Mellor transform symbols, which are circles, are also considered rectangular.

Lines (a.k.a. line symbols) have predefined characteristics such as straight or arced shapes, arrowheads or crow's feet for beginning or end points, and, in certain methodologies, indicators of cardinality. These characteristics are called associative properties.

Table 2-1 discusses the similarities and differences in the generic characteristics of rectangular and line symbols:

Characteristic	Rectangular Symbol	Line Symbol
Size	can be modified	can be modified
Predefined characteristics	Shape	Shape (straight or arced) - can be modified, Cardinality indicators (arrowheads, crow's feet, etc.) - can be modified
Display properties	Name, Number, Graphic Comment, Key and Non-key data	Name, Graphic Comment
Attachments	A Rectangular symbol may have zero or more lines attached to it.	A line may be attached to a rectangular symbol at one or both ends, or it may be detached at both ends.
Moving Symbol	Rectangular symbols can be moved around the screen individually or as a group.	If attached, line can be moved one end at a time by dragging a handle; the line segment "rubberbands". A segment automatically "rubberbands" to accommodate movement of the attached symbol. If detached at both ends, it may be moved as a "block" without changing its shape.
Handles (appear when symbol is selected)	Solid square handles appear in the corners, and the center of each side.	Handles are cross-shaped at the point the line is attached to another symbol, and solid squares at connections of line segments.
Hidden Comment	Each instance of a symbol may also have a unique but hidden comment attached to it.	

Table 2-1. Characteristics of Symbols

2.3.2 Characteristics of Labels

You should be aware of the following generic characteristics of labels (names and numbers):

- A name, or label, is attached to a rectangular symbol or line. This name is specified in a dialog box that pops up when the symbol or line is first placed (when the **Auto Name** default is on). A name can be any combination of 31 keyboard characters.

- Rectangular Symbol labels are automatically placed within the symbol unless the default settings are modified using **Text Position** command in the **Set** menu. The symbol can be automatically resized if the text does not fit inside the symbol, or you can decrease the size of the text font.

- Line labels are automatically centered above the middle line segment. When the line is selected, the label can be moved simply by dragging it to a new location. If the default **Auto Reposition Name** is on, the label snaps to the original position each time the line or an attached symbol is moved.

2.4 Logical Characteristics of Diagrams

You should be aware of the following generic characteristics of diagrams:

- All graphic objects on a diagram are referred to as symbols.

- Each symbol on a diagram conveys information to the person studying it. The symbols form a graphic language of their own. This language is discussed in its methodological context in the mini-tutorials.

- Other logical characteristics of diagrams include the existence of hidden information that is accessible from the diagrams. This information can take the form of relationships between diagrams (referred to as leveling) or relationships between definitions (known as the data dictionary).

2.4.1 Leveling

Leveling, or creating a hierarchy of related diagram-levels, solves the problem of assigning too much detail to any one diagram.

The concept of leveling is traditionally associated with Data Flow diagrams; a process symbol can be "decomposed" or "exploded" into its components at a lower level. The hierarchy hides detail at the upper levels to describe the context of the system, and shows it at the lower levels as a result of specifying a smaller piece of the system.

System Architect allows leveling of any logical entity, whether it is a process, a data store, or a symbol of some other methodology altogether. The concept of leveling is generalized so that it can be applied equally to all methodologies and all symbols. This flexibility allows the user to divide any specification into a series of levels. In addition, for certain methodologies, System Architect allows you to verify that the parent symbol balances with respect to its child diagram. Generally speaking, balancing means to check the inputs and outputs of a diagram against the corresponding inputs and outputs of the symbol in the diagram at the previous level (the parent). The concepts of balancing and rules checking are covered in a mini-tutorial.

System Architect also supports the "bottom-up" approach, which calls for documenting all the details known about a system, and grouping these details into logical units that can be shown to interact with other grouped structures. Existing diagrams of processing at lower levels can be built into a hierarchy by attaching (and detaching) them together in the correct order.

2.4.2 Storing Definitions

All your symbol definitions are stored in the project encyclopedia's data dictionary. The data dictionary provides a centralized repository for information that is equally accessible to all diagrams sharing the same encyclopedia.

The data dictionary is a logical construct within the System Architect Encyclopedia consisting of symbol definitions and related data. Every symbol on any type of diagram has a corresponding definition type and potential definition. System Architect uses a few basic concepts that apply to all methodologies to create definitions and relationships in the data dictionary.

2.4.3 Dictionary Entries

System Architect extends the strict definition of a data dictionary to include Process descriptions, Module specifications, Requirement definitions, Test Plans, and many others.

Each dictionary entry is identified by name and definition type. Examples of definition types include *process, data store, entity,* and so on. Any given name must be unique within each definition type. When two graphic symbols have the same name and map to the same definition type, they are logically connected to one dictionary definition. As an example, the *ISBN Master List* data store symbol appears on three different diagrams, but there is only one dictionary entry, which defines all three symbols.

A data element and a data structure may not have the same name -- they are not different definitions, but the same: *data*. The same name, however, can be used for a process, a data flow, a data store, and so on.

Dictionary Descriptions

For most definition types the description, defined as free form text, is the first property or characteristic to define the dictionary entry. For classic data types such as data flows, data stores, data structures, and data flags, a syntax called an "expression statement" is used. Expression statements implement a Yourdon standard. The term *expression* indicates that a pre-defined syntax is required for the definition of the data type. The syntax is a convention for accurately specifying the relationships between the components of a data expression. Components in a data expression are either data elements or data structures.

Other definition types may use different statements. For example, a process, as you will see in the example of *ISBN Master List* is defined as a *Minispec*.

Data Domains

A *data domain* can be used to specify default physical properties to be shared by a group of data elements. The data domain property set is always a subset of the data element property set.

Data Elements

A *data element* is the smallest unit of stored data, which means that it cannot be broken down further, or that it makes no sense to break it down further. The default properties for a group of data elements can, however, be specified by a data domain. Elements are defined (described) by characteristics, referred to in System Architect as properties.

Data Structures

Data Structures are convenient groupings of data (elements and/or other structures), and can be defined by expressing the components in a precise syntax.

Expression Syntax

The expression syntax in its simplest form can be read as "Data Expression A is composed of Component_B and Component_C and..." In the case just described where one or more components are needed to form a data structure, the syntax is called a sequence structure. Other types of relationships can also be shown in data expressions. These syntax structures are written using a shorthand of keyboard characters surrounding the components to indicate the type of structure:

> {...}
>
>> *iteration:* Multiple iterations of the enclosed component are available. A lower limit may be specified as a numeric prefix and an upper limit may be specified as a numeric suffix. These numeric limits are placed outside the structure braces; e.g., 1{order_line}5
>
> (...)
>
>> *option:* The enclosed component is optional.
>
> [B | C]
>
>> *choice:* The Data Expression is composed of Component B or Component C
>
> @n   where n is a number 1-999
>
>> *key:* The component acts as the key or part of a compound key in the data structure The @ sign or @n may be written directly next to the component, or they may be separated by a space for increased readability.
>
>> ```
>> @ ISBN
>> ```
>
> or
>
>> ```
>> @1 ISBN +
>> @2 Customer_ID
>> ```

To determine the nature of the data expression for ISBN Master List, you can first think of a verbal description. An entry in the ISBN card catalog system usually lists pertinent information on a book; this information is cross-referenced by subject, title, and author, in addition to where the book can be found. More formally you could state the structure:

> A Data Store called **ISBN Master List**
> *is composed of* **a list of subjects or categories**
> *and* **some information on the book's title, author, publisher, copyright date,**
> *and* **some information on the book's index and bibliography**

Syntax Rules

Data element and data structure names used in an expression must adhere to stricter naming conventions than symbol names because System Architect must distinguish the component as a unit and check for proper syntax. Syntactical errors are flagged in the expression check; an error message assists you in locating the violation. The following rules will help you avoid these errors:

- Spaces are used to separate components of a data expression; therefore, to create a compound name you must use a hyphen character, an underscore character, or enclose the compound name in double quotes to connect the components of the name (e.g., *Author-Name* or *Author_Name* or *"Author Name"*).

- A "+" character may appear between any two components (or between the syntactical structures of the components as described above) in *ExpressionOf* statements. The "+" signs are optional.

- Asterisks (*) may be used to separate and enclose a comment from the remainder of the syntax.

- Data expression component names must begin with an alphabetic character, although numeric characters may be contained elsewhere in the name.

- Special characters, other than those with a syntactical function, are not permitted unless enclosed in double quotes.

☞ *It is not necessary to enter carriage returns between the elements in an expression, but they make a complex expression easier to read. After all, communication is one of the chief goals of CASE methods.*

Checking Expression Syntax

System Architect checks the syntax of your expression, and determines if any of the components of your expression are undefined, when you click the **Check** button or click **OK** to save and exit the definition dialog. If the expression uses undefined data, System Architect asks if you would like to retain a list of the undefined components. Click **Yes** or **No**, as you prefer. If errors exist in the syntax of your expression, System Architect displays an error message.

All errors must be corrected before the definition can be saved.

2.4.4 Definition Type Properties

Properties are assigned for each definition type, and are included in the dictionary definition dialog to permit capture of specific information for each occurrence. The properties are equivalent to fields in a database, each having certain edit requirements to control the quality and format of the collected information. These edits might specify a numeric value, or limit the length of a text string. The property may even provide a multiple choice list of appropriate responses to eliminate unnecessary text entry. The properties set creates a custom application screen to capture data for each dictionary definition type or category.

2.4.5 Definition Types

System Architect supports over 100 different symbols for the different diagrams and methodologies. But there are fewer definition types, because several different symbol types often map to a single definition type. For example, a *process symbol* on a Gane & Sarson diagram and a *data transform symbol* on a Ward & Mellor diagram both map to the definition type process.

Most, but not all, of the definition types are derived from the symbol types on the diagrams, such as "data flow" definitions, "data store" definitions, and "process" definitions. A definition data name categorized as one of these types corresponds one-to-one with the same name and symbol type on the diagrams. These types are described in the mini-tutorial describing the related methodology.

Types not derived from the diagrams are method-independent and might be used in association with many diagram types. Specifications (*Requirements, Test Plans, Change Requests, etc.*) and *Glossary* items fit this list, in addition to *Data Structures, Data Elements, and Data Domains*. Another type that is derived from the diagrams but remains method-independent is the *Comment.* Specifications and Comments are described briefly below.

Specifications

Some data types are used by the dictionary to classify or relate data to the diagram symbols. Specifications such as *Requirements, Test Plans*, and *Change Requests* express a relationship of one name to many symbols, or many names to one symbol. These particular definition types are described in greater detail as they are used in this tutorial.

Comments

A *Comment* is a free-form text field description that documents a single occurrence of a graphic symbol. Comments are limited to 4,095 characters. For a symbol which has a comment attached, three dots (expand indicators) appear, with the left expand indicator filled black.

The *Graphic Comment* also documents a single instance of a symbol, but it is limited to 1000 characters and can be displayed on a diagram.

2.5 Questions In Review

1. What is an **Audit ID**? What are its characteristics?

2. What would be the name of the encyclopedia which resided in the directory C:\SYSARCH\PROJECT1? How many encyclopedias can be created in the Student Version of System Architect?

3. What menu and command would you use to modify your session's preference settings?

4. How can a data domain be used?

5. Define and compare Data Elements and Data Structures.

6. What is the syntax called for the following expression:
   "Data Expression A is composed of Component_B and Component_C and...".

7. Why must data element and data structure names used in an expression adhere to stricter naming conventions than symbol names?

8. System Architect supports over 100 different symbols types, but fewer definition types, why?

9. What is a System Architect comment?

10. What is a System Architect graphic comment?

Answers to the above questions can be found in Appendix B.

3. Process Modeling

Process modeling is a technique for describing the functional characteristics of a system. It involves the flow and transformation of data through the various processes of the system and the functional decomposition of these processes. Functional decomposition is a hierarchical method of reducing a complex system into understandable parts; these parts are then described in greater detail at each level of the hierarchy. The process model uses a graphic language to diagram information (data) as it circulates (flows) and is transformed throughout a system. Thus the term "Data Flow Diagramming" has become almost synonymous with "process modeling." System Architect supports four types of data flow diagrams: Gane & Sarson, Ward & Mellor, Yourdon/DeMarco, and SSADM IV. Our example uses the Gane & Sarson approach.

Reasons for using the process-modeling approach include:

- It provides a means for understanding complex systems.

- It provides a means for evaluating system requirements.

- It provides a simple and accurate language/method for communication between the clients, the users, and the development team.

- It provides a basis for the physical design.

- It creates a machine-readable repository of data that can evolve through later development stages and be used in the generation of the software.

Using a graphic language for describing systems replaces the cumbersome and inefficient method of documenting systems with pages and pages of narrative text. In addition to being a clear, fast documentation strategy, data flow diagrams are tools for analysts to visualize relationships that otherwise would be obscured in ambiguous text.

3.1 Overview

The actual "how to do analysis" is much too large a topic to be dealt with in the context of learning to use System Architect. The concept of extracting the logical functioning of a system from the current physical implementation (or proposed system) is, however, the first and critical stage of structured analysis. The analysis of a current system (or the requirements for a proposed system) must interpret and model only the essential transformations (processes), independent of any assumed or existing physical environment such as computer hardware or coding language. Only essential and inflexible physical details, such as certain material flows that are part of the system definition, should be included in the analysis stage. For data flow diagrams to be effective as analysis tools they should be clear of any reference to implementation decisions.

Various diagramming styles of process modeling have evolved from the developers and writers of the original theory; their differences are less important than their similarities. Each of the methodologies uses a few powerful yet straightforward concepts, and a very simple symbol set, to represent the functional view of a system. These symbols and concepts are described briefly in *Table 3-1*. A general description of the symbol type is also provided in *Table 3-1*.

In addition to describing systems graphically, process modeling requires that a diagram remain simple enough to be understood quickly, and not contain details that could more appropriately be put elsewhere. In real terms, this means that a diagram should contain no more than about one page of symbols and data flows, and ideally have a maximum of 7 process symbols. It is possible to keep the diagrams simple and clear while documenting all the necessary detail using a leveled set of DFDs. Our examples use the Gane & Sarson symbol set.

Gane & Sarson	Ward & Mellor	Yourdon/ DeMarco	SSADM Context/DFD	Description
P1 Process	P1 Data Transform; P1 Multi Control Transform; Also, Multi Data Transform, and Control Transform	P1 Process	System (Context); 1 Process (DFD)	The *Process*, or *Data Transform*, is used to convert the input data to output data. The symbol represents the actions necessary to complete the conversion.
D1 Data Store; D1 Multi Data Store	D1 Data Store; D1 Control Store	D1 Data Store	D1 Data Store; T1 Transient Data Store; M1 Manual Data Store (DFD only)	*Data Stores* are used to indicate that information is being stored until it is needed by another process. A data store is an inventory of data.
External; Multi External	External	External	External	A system must have boundaries in order to be clearly defined. The fourth symbol, called an *External* (or terminator), simply indicates anything outside the scope of the current system.
Data Flow; Material Flow	Discrete Flow; Continuous Flow; Event Flow	Data Flow	Data Flow	*Data Flows* indicate the movement of data between symbols.

Table 3-1. Data Flow Diagrams and Symbol Types

3.2 Drawing a Context Diagram

Drawing diagrams with System Architect is quick and easy. However, the steps for placing symbols and drawing lines may be different from other drawing products with which you may be familiar.

Take a moment to study the following instructions. The practices you are accustomed to using with other packages may not be correct for System Architect. We will be using the Gane & Sarson style for all of the data flow diagrams we will be using in this manual. The Gane & Sarson methodology is one of a group generally referred to as Structured Analysis and Design. Refer to *Table 3-1* for other data flow diagramming techniques supported by System Architect.

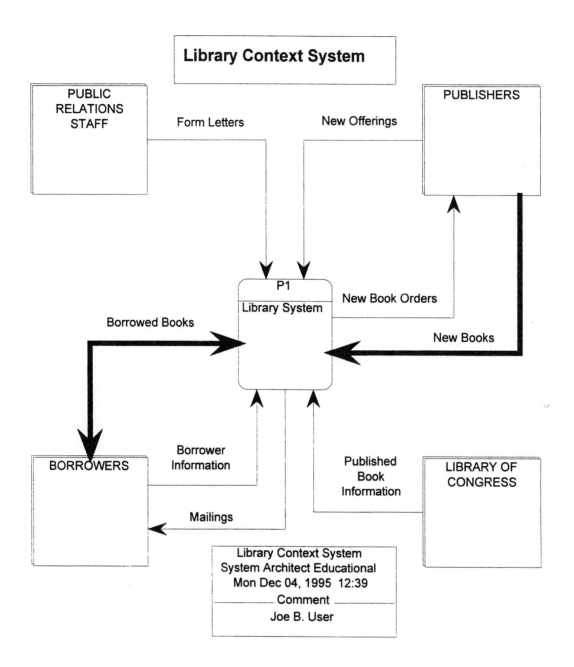

Figure 3-1. The Library Context Diagram

A *context diagram* is the top-most data flow diagram (DFD) in structured analysis. It usually consists of a single process symbol at the center of the page, surrounded by external entity symbols or "terminators" that feed data into the system and receive data from it. This process represents *the System*; thus, it is generally named for the system being analyzed (*Library System*).

In this section we are going to begin creating the context level DFD for the Library System as shown in *Figure 3-1*.

1. Pull down the **Diagram** Menu and select the **New** command.

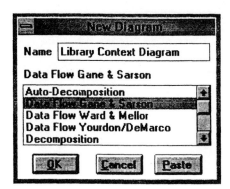

Figure 3-2. Preparing to Create a New Diagram

2. In the **Name** box type Library Context Diagram.

3. Select the diagram type **Data Flow Gane & Sarson** from the diagram selection box below the **Name** box.

4. Click on the **OK** button. A blank drawing screen appears.

All menus except **Symbol** are now active, the **Symbol** menu is only active when a symbol has been selected. The **DFD-GS** methodology menu now appears on the far right of the menu bar. It contains the symbol and line drawing commands you need to draw diagrams matching the Gane & Sarson data flow diagram standard; those symbols are also accessible from the toolbox, displayed in the left margin of the window.

3.2.1 The System Architect Window

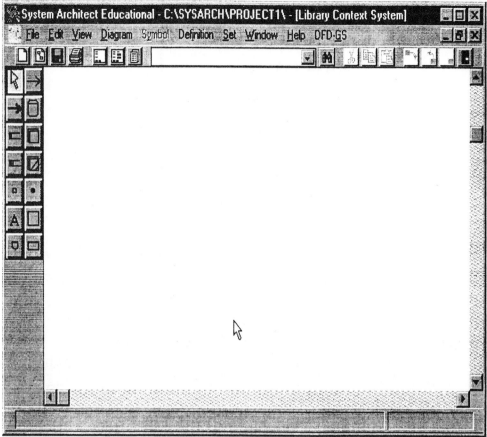

Figure 3-3. System Architect Window

System Architect provides a *Toolbar* and a *Toolbox*.

The Toolbar

Figure 3-4. The Toolbar

The System Architect toolbar appears below the menu bar at the top of the
System Architect window. The icons may be used to perform common drawing
functions. The name of each icon can be displayed by slowly moving the mouse
pointer over the icon.

The table on the next page shows the icon, the menu equivalent, and a brief
explanation of the action each performs.

Icon	Menu command	Action
	Diagram Menu New	Start a new diagram
	Diagram Menu Open	Open an existing diagram
	Diagram Menu Save	Save the diagram currently in focus
	File Menu Print	Print the diagram currently in focus
	Definition Menu Add	Add a new definition for any object supported by System Architect
	Definition Menu Modify	Modify any definition in the encyclopedia
	File Menu Reports	Load the report file in preparation for selecting a report to run.
FORM LETTER (Entity)	N/A	the Symbol Locate list box
	N/A	Rapid Locate
	Edit Menu Cut	Cut selected symbols from the diagram currently in focus.
	Edit Menu Copy	Copy selected symbols from the diagram currently in focus.
	Edit Menu Paste	Paste selected symbols or text from the Clipboard to the diagram in focus.
	Symbol Menu Child Open	Open and change focus to the child diagram of the currently selected symbol.
	Symbol Menu Parent	Open and change focus to the diagram of the parent symbol of the diagram currently in focus.
	Symbol Menu Top	Open and change focus to the diagram at the top of the leveled set of the diagram currently in focus.
	View Menu Toolbox	Toggle the Toolbox on and off. (This command affects diagrams of the type currently in focus.)
	Edit Menu Route now	Route any selected lines of the Automatic orthogonal style.

Table 3-2. Icons on the Toolbar

Symbol Locate

The Symbol Locate list box can be used in two ways. If a symbol is selected, its name and type is displayed in the box. On the other hand, if you want to rapidly locate any symbol on a diagram, find its name in the list and select it. Then click on the binoculars. The focus of the diagram immediately shifts to the chosen symbol. The chosen view size of the diagram does not change.

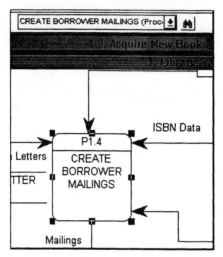

Figure 3-5. The name and symbol type in the Symbol Locate list box

The Toolbox

There is a unique Toolbox for every methodology menu. The tools in the Toolbox are specific to the methodology.

Figure 3-6. Toolbox for the Gane & Sarson Data Flow Diagram

You can toggle the Toolbox on and off for individual diagrams by

- de-selecting **Toolbox** from the **View** menu,

- de-selecting **Toolbox** from the floating diagram menu[1], or
- clicking the Toolbox icon on the Toolbar.

The *Display Toolbox Preference* must be toggled on for the toolbox to be opened automatically with the diagram.

3.2.2 Window Size

Most people prefer drawing diagrams on a large screen. Click on the "maximize" button to obtain the largest possible work area

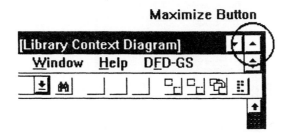

Figure 3-7. The Maximize Button

3.2.3 Reduction Percentage

When beginning a new diagram, System Architect will, by default, display the actual size of the symbols on the screen. When you're drawing a large diagram, the Actual Size option may not allow you to show a significant portion of the diagram on your screen, and clarity may be lost with the **Used Area** option such that you can't determine the names of your symbols.

You will often find drawing easier if you work on a moderately reduced scale. From experience, we have found that a 75% reduction usually works well. This is the System Architect default value for the reduced view. To change to 75% reduction:

---

[1] For information about floating menus, refer to *Section 5.6, Using Popup Menus*.

1. Pull down the **View** menu.

2. Click on **Reduced 75%**.

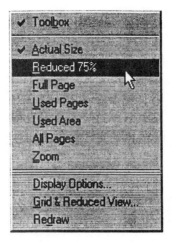

Figure 3-8. The **View** Menu

The percentage of reduction for the **Reduce *n*%** command (**Reduce 75%** in our example) is specified using the **Grid & Reduced View** command.

3.2.3.1 Setting the Reduced View Percentage

The Grid & Reduced View command is used to change the percentage for reducing the view.

The following procedure is used to specify the reduction percentage:

1. Pull down the **View** menu.

2. Click on the **Grid & Reduced View** command. The **Grid & Reduced View Settings** dialog appears.

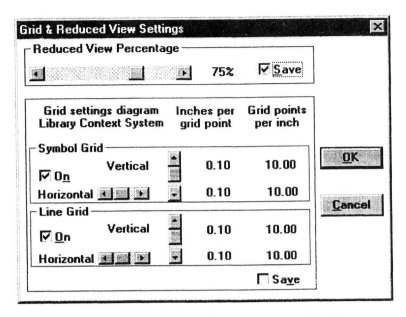

Figure 3-9. Grid & Reduced View Dialog

3. The horizontal scroll bar in the **Reduced View Percentage** box can be used to specify the percent reduction for the **Reduce _n_%** command in the **View** menu. We will leave this at the default value of 75%.

4. Click on **Save** in the **Reduced View Percentage** box to use the specified percent reduction as the default setting.

5. Click on **OK**.

3.2.4 Drawing Symbols

All rectangular symbols are drawn and placed on the diagram in the same way.

Hint Slowly drag your cursor over the Toolbox, without pressing the mouse button. The name of the symbol under the cursor is displayed in a small rectangle to the right of the icon of the tool. The Toolbar works the same way, displaying the action of the icon.

1. Pull down the **DFD-GS** menu and select _Process_, or select the Process symbol from the Toolbox.

The cursor changes to a "pencil and rectangle." The pencil indicates you are in "draw" mode, ready to place symbols in your diagram. The rectangle tells you that you will be placing a rectangular shaped symbol; a process symbol in this case.[2]

---

2 In System Architect, the term "rectangular symbol" is used to indicate symbols that are not linear.

Figure 3-10. Cursor in Draw Mode

2. Move the cursor to the approximate place on the drawing area where you would like your symbol to appear and press on the left mouse button. A process symbol appears above and to the left of the cursor. Do not release the mouse button.

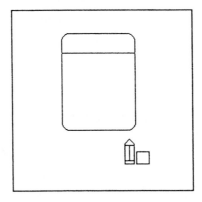

Figure 3-11. The process symbol and the cursor in its drawing shape

Continue to hold down the left button and move the mouse, "dragging" the process symbol across the screen. Notice that the symbol moves with the mouse.

Hint System Architect orients the symbol on an invisible grid as you move it. For information on how to set the grid size, please refer to information on the **View** Menu, **Display Options** Submenu, **Grid & Reduced View** Command in the On-line Help.

3. Drag the process symbol to the center of the visible portion of the diagram and release the mouse button, anchoring it.

   If you want to move the symbol after it's anchored, see *Section 5.1, Moving Symbols.*

4. The **Add Symbol (Process)** dialog box is displayed since the **Auto Name** option is set on in the **Preferences** dialog. Type Library System in the **Name** text box.

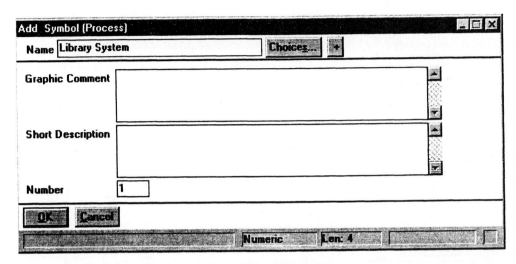

Figure 3-12. Enter the name in the **Add Symbol [Process]** Dialog Box

5. Type the following description in the **Short Description** text box:

This system is designed to:

A. Track books that have been lent to borrowers.

B. Increase the speed with which new books are added to the libraries.

C. Reduce theft of books.

6. Click on **OK**.

7. The **Add Definition (Process)** dialog is displayed. The context level diagram doesn't need a minispec, so click the right-pointing arrow in the lower right-hand corner, to move to the second page of the definition dialog.

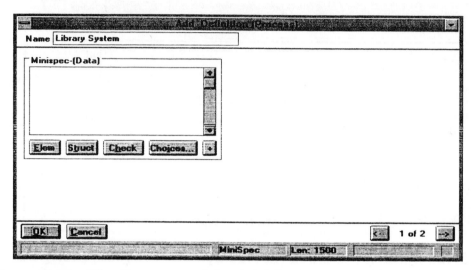

Figure 3-13. The first page of the **Add Definition (Process)** dialog

8. Enter the descriptive text in the **Purpose** text box as shown in *Figure 3-14*, and click on **OK** to save the definition.

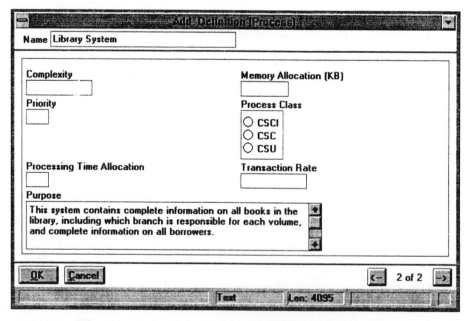

Figure 3-14. The second page of the **Add Definition (Process)** dialog

To continue adding symbols to your diagram, take the following steps:

1.  Change to a different symbol type, the *external entity*, by clicking on the **DFD-GS** menu and selecting the **External** command, or by selecting from the Toolbox. The cursor remains a "pencil and rectangle."

   Move the External Entity to the area roughly above the upper left-hand corner of the process symbol. Place it, and name it PUBLIC RELATIONS STAFF.

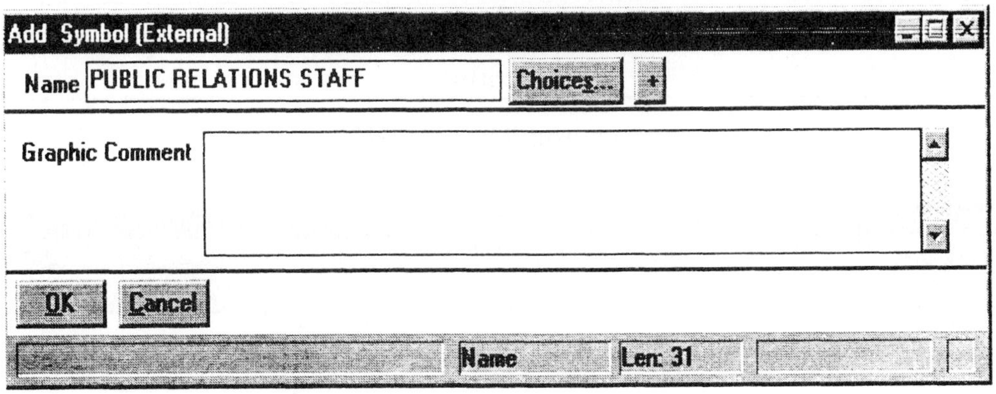

Figure 3-15. Add Symbol dialog

2. Click on **OK**.

3. Enter the descriptive information about the PR staff in the Description text box of the **Modify Definition (External)** dialog as shown in *Figure 3-16*. Click on **OK**.

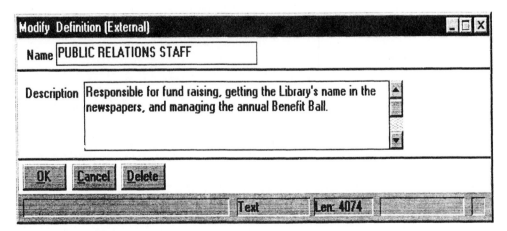

Figure 3-16. Adding a Symbol description

4. Place and name three more External Entities listed in the table below. It is not necessary to capitalize the name of External Entities. You should follow the naming convention of your project or company.

Entity Name	Description
PUBLISHERS	Organizations which supply books to the library.
BORROWERS	Individuals who check out books.
LIBRARY OF CONGRESS	Governing body which assigns ISBN numbers.

Table 3-3. Entities and Their Descriptions

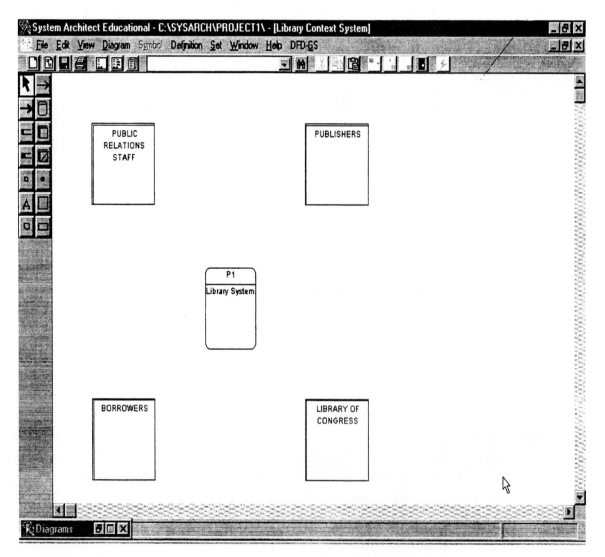

Figure 3-17. Draw Three More External Entities

There are some general hints about editing, selecting and moving symbols that may be useful. They have all been gathered in *Section 5, Editing Symbols and Lines*.

3.3 Printing The Diagram

The **Print** command allows the user to print the current diagram to a specified printer.

To print the *Library Context System* diagram currently displayed in the active window:

1. Pull down the **File** menu and select the **Print** command.

2. The diagram is sent to the printer.

☞ *Please note that the printer options that are changed in System Architect using the **Page Setup** dialog in the **File** menu are not permanent changes to the printer setup. Your printer setup is controlled by Windows.*

3.4 Saving a Diagram

Save your work frequently, using the **Save** command from the **Diagram** menu, or the **Save Diagram** button on the toolbar. Changes to a diagram are not recorded in the encyclopedia until the diagram is saved. Therefore, if you were to lose power to your PC, all the work you have done since opening the diagram (or from your last save) will be lost.

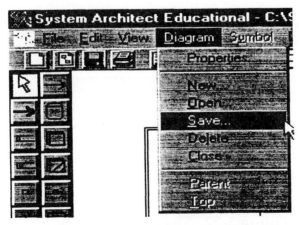

Figure 3-19. The **Diagram** Menu

3.5 Exiting System Architect

There are three ways to exit System Architect:

- Pull down the **File** menu, and click on the **Exit** command.

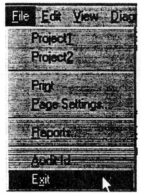

Figure 3-20. The **File** Menu

- Double-click on the *Control-menu box*.

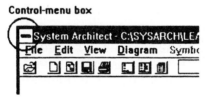

Figure 3-21. The Control-Menu Box

- Single-click on the *Control-menu box*, then click on the **Close** command in the Control menu.

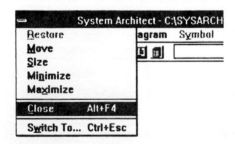

Figure 3-22. The Control Menu

3.6   Questions in Review

1. Define the process modeling technique.

2. List three reasons for using the process-modeling approach.

3. What is a context diagram and what does it consist of?

4. What is the **DFD-GS** methodology menu?

5. Name three ways to toggle the Toolbox on and off for individual diagrams.

6. When the cursor changes to a "pencil and rectangle", what does that indicate?

7. Which menu and command would you use to increase the number of grid points per inch?

8. What two techniques can you use to save your diagram?

9. If you were to lose power to your PC, would all the work you have done, either creating or modifying a diagram, be lost since opening the diagram (or from your last save)?

10. List three ways to exit System Architect.

Answers to the above questions can be found in Appendix B.

4. Completing The Context Diagram

In this section we are going to finish the context level DFD for the Library
System started in Chapter 3. The diagram is shown in *Figure 4-1*.

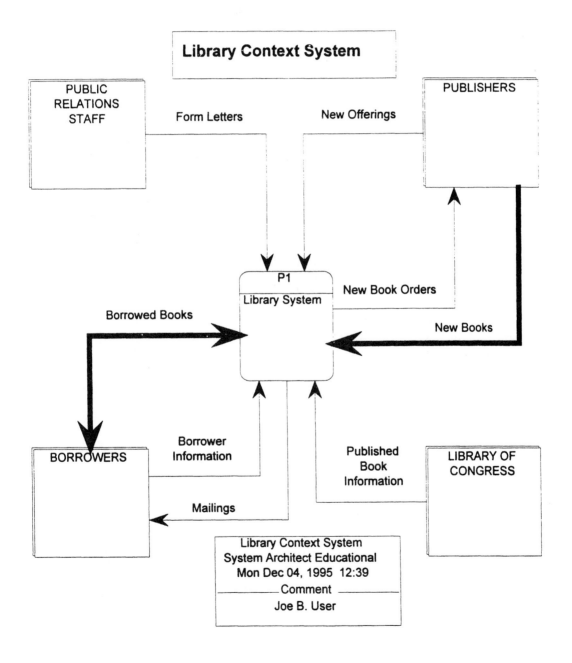

Figure 4-1. The Library System Context Level DFD

4.1 Opening a Diagram

This section assumes you have started System Architect and opened the *Project1* encyclopedia. If you haven't, please do so at this time.

1. Pull down the **Diagram** menu and click **Open**. The **Select For Opening** dialog will be displayed. Click **Search**.

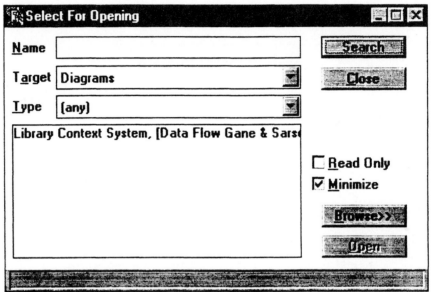

Figure 4-2. The Open Diagram Dialog

2. System Architect will search for all diagrams of any type and list them in the text box. Select the *Library Context System* diagram and click **Open**.

The Library Context System diagram is displayed.

4.2 Drawing Lines Connecting Symbols

Lines connecting symbols have different meanings, depending on the modeling method chosen. In data flow diagrams, for example, lines are called *data flows* and represent the movement of data (elements) through a system.

In System Architect the techniques for drawing all lines, regardless of the methodology you are using and what is represented, are the same.

4.2.1 Available Line Types

System Architect supports four different line types. The differences are summarized in this table:

Cursor shape when selected	Line type	Characteristics
	Straight, any orientation	Does not require bend points, but lines can be bent at any angle.[1]
	Straight orthogonal	To switch direction must have 1 or more bend points.[2]
	Automatic orthogonal	Exactly like straight orthogonal, but System Architect determines the bend points for you.
	Elliptical arc	Curved line between rectangular symbols.

Table 4-1. Supported Line Styles

The Gane & Sarson diagram notation standard calls for all data flow line segments to be horizontal or vertical; this goal can be obtained using either the *Straight - orthogonal* or *Automatic (orthogonal)* line style. We will use *Straight (orthogonal)* lines for this example. You can specify this as the default *line style*. Once set, System Architect will not allow you to draw data flow lines on the diagonal, until you re-specify the line style. To set your line style default:

1. Pull down the **Set** menu.

2. Choose the **Line** command.

3. Set the **Straight - orthogonal** option to **ON**.

4. Ensure the **Round Corners** option is **not** checked.

5. Set the **Save** option to **ON**; the new setting will be saved as the default setting.

6. Click on **OK**.

---

[1] If you're familiar with the game of chess, this line type moves like the Queen, it that it can go any direction it wants (providing a bendpoint is placed where the direction is changed).

[2] This line type moves like the rook, it can go straight across, but requires a bendpoint to change direction.

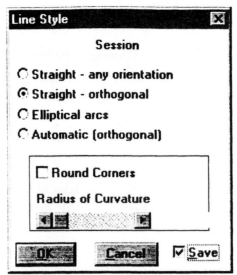

Figure 4-3. The **Line Style** Dialog

4.2.2 Drawing Data Flow Lines

To draw a straight line connecting the *PUBLIC RELATIONS STAFF* and
Library System symbols:

1. Pull down the **DFD-GS** menu and select the **Data Flow** command
    or select the line symbol from the Toolbox.

    You will notice that the cursor now has changed to the "draw"
    mode indicator "pencil" shape. Notice the cross next to the pencil,
    indicating the straight orthogonal line.

2. Place the pencil point *inside* the symbol from which you want the line to
    start. It is not necessary to try to start the line precisely on the side of
    the symbol; place it well inside the symbol and System Architect will
    make sure it is connected.

3. *Press and hold down* the mouse button. A movable handle in the shape
    of a cross appears on one side of the symbol. Do not release the mouse
    button.

    If the handle is inside the symbol, it appears as a cross. If it is outside
    the symbol, it appears as a box.

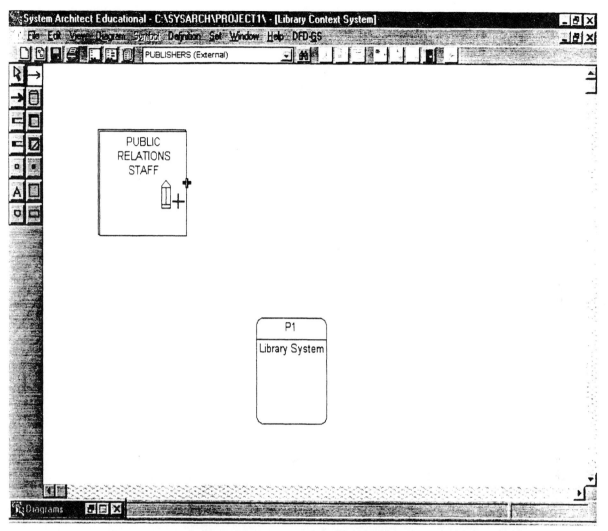

Figure 4-4. Start to Draw the Line from *Inside* the Starting Symbol

4. Continue to hold down the mouse button and move the cursor around inside the symbol. The handle on the symbol boundary will move around the edge line as you move the cursor. When you have moved the handle to the symbol perimeter line from which you want the data flow to start, release the mouse button.

☞ *If you want to stop drawing a line before you have attached it at both ends to a symbol, press the Escape key. The line disappears and the cursor changes to a pointer shape. To begin another line, you will have to select the* **Data Flow** *command again.*

Notice that when you drag the mouse from the source symbol towards the target symbol, the line only moves in a straight direction -- it does not bend.

5. Move the cursor to the right, dragging the line straight across to a point to the right of the *Public Relations* external entity symbol, directly over the *Library System* process symbol.

6. Click the left mouse button.

   A new bend point handle appears, anchoring the first line segment at that point. The next line segment can now continue in a new direction from the bend point.

7. Pull the line down, until the pencil shape is inside the process symbol.

   Hold the left mouse button down, and move the mouse until the cross at the end of the data flow line is directly over *P1*. Release the mouse button.

Hint For every bend point, click the left mouse button once. You can have as many bend points as are required to make the line look the way you want it to. As you continue to work on your diagram, you can add more bend points or take them away, as necessary. See *Section 5.2, Modifying Lines*.

Once you release the left mouse button, the **Add Symbol (Data Flow)** dialog appears. Now you can add a name and properties to the data flow.

1. Type the name Form Letters in the **Name** box.

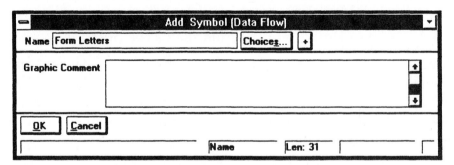

Figure 4-5. Naming a Data Flow

2. Click on **OK**.

3. The **Add Definition (Data Flow)** dialog is displayed, in which are entered the attributes, or data, carried on the data flow line. Enter the data element name Form-Letter-ID in the **Data** text box.

4. Hit the enter key to move the cursor to the next line.

5. Enter the second data element name, Form-Letter-Text.

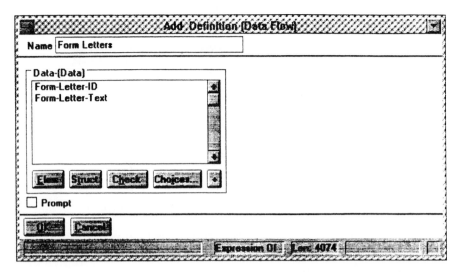

Figure 4-6. The **Add Definition [Data Flow]** Dialog

6. Select the words *Form-Letter-ID* in the data text box, and click on the *Elem* button at the bottom of the box.

7. The **Add Definition (Data Element)** dialog is displayed. Enter the description in the Description text box as shown in *Figure 4-7*, and click on **OK**.

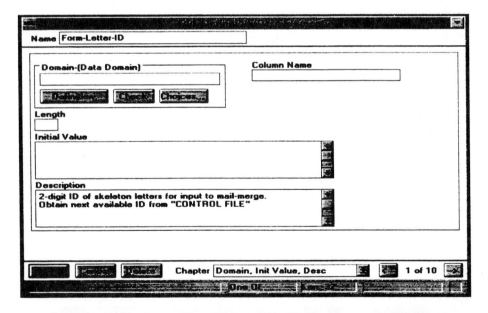

Figure 4-7. The **Add Definition (Data Element)** Dialog

8. Repeat steps 6 and 7 for the second data element, *Form-Letter-Text* with the description, Skeleton letters in format suitable for mail merge.

9. Once the data elements have been defined, select **OK** in the **Add Definition (Data Flow)** window.

10. The **Associative Properties** dialog is displayed

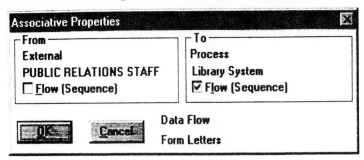

Figure 4-8. The **Associative Property** Dialog

This dialog allows you to select the flow direction of the data flow line. The check box containing the check will be the end of the data flow containing the arrowhead.

11. Select **OK**.

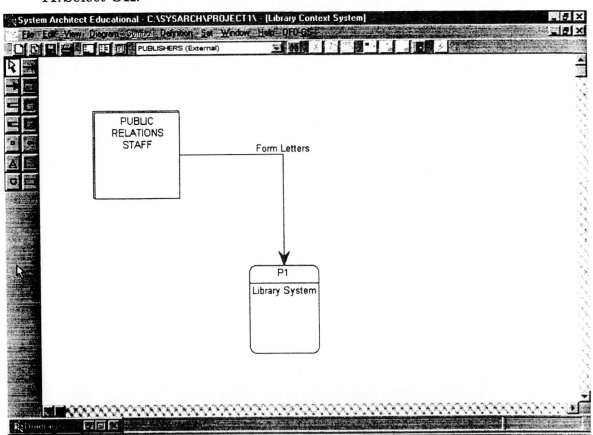

Figure 4-9. A completed line in the straight orthogonal style

The arrowhead color is black because the line is connected to a rectangular symbol at both ends.

☞ *A line that is attached at both ends to symbols has a **black arrowhead**. A line that is attached at only one end to a symbol has a **hatched arrowhead**, that is, a partially filled-in arrowhead. A line that is not attached at either end to a symbol has a **white arrowhead**.*

The arrowhead color is a visual cue that the line is fully attached to symbols at both ends. It is possible to have lines that are attached to a symbol at only one end, or to have free-standing lines.

12. Repeat the add data flow process to add the remaining data flows to the diagram shown in *Figure 4.1*. The following tables 4-2 through 4-4 contain the definitions needed to define the flows.

    Please note some of the data flows contain data structures which are group names for a set of data elements. For example, *Borrower-Name* is a data structure which contains the data elements, *Borrower-Last-Name, Borrower-First-Name* and *Borrower-Middle-Init*. Data structures are defined by selecting the data name, then clicking the **Struct** button. This will display another **Add Definition (Data Flow)** window in which to enter the structure's data elements. Each data element will then need to be selected and the **Elem** button clicked in order to add the definition.

Definition	Contains	
Borrower Information	data element	Borrower-ID
	data structure	Borrower-Name
	data structure	Borrower-Address-Block
	data structure	References
	data structure	Reserve-Book-Data
New Offerings	data element	ISBN
	data element	Title
	data element	Author-Name
	data element	Publisher
	data element	Copyright-Date
	data element	Biblography-Indic
	data element	Index-Indic
	data element	Subject-Category
New Book Orders	data element	ISBN
	data element	Title
	data element	Author-Name
	data element	Publisher
	data element	Copyright-Date
	data element	Quantity-Ordered
Mailings	data element	Complete-Letter-Text
	data structure	Borrower-Name
	data structure	Borrower-Address-Block

Definition	Contains	
Published Book Information	data element	ISBN
	data element	Title
	data element	Author-Name
	data element	Publisher
	data element	Copyright-Date
	data element	Subject-Category

Table 4-2. Data on the data flows in the Library Context Diagram

Data Structure	Contains these data elements
Borrower-Name	Borrower-Last-Name Borrower-First-Name Borrower-Middle-Init
Borrower-Address-Block	Borrower-House Borrower-Street Borrower-City Borrower-State Borrower-ZIP
References	Reference-Name Reference-Address-Block Reference-Description
Reference-Address-Block	Reference-House Reference-Street Reference-City Reference-State Reference-ZIP
Reserve-Book-Data	ISBN Date-Requested

Table 4-3. Data Structure definitions

Data Element	Description
Author-Name	Author of book
Bibliography-Indic	Does this book have a bibliography?
Borrower-City	self-explanatory
Borrower-First-Name	self-explanatory
Borrower-House	Borrower house number.
Borrower-ID	If possible, user borrower's SSN else use the next available ID.
Borrower-Last-Name	self-explanatory
Borrower-Middle-Init	self-explanatory
Borrower-State	Use standard postal 2-letter codes.
Borrower-Street	self-explanatory

Data Element	Description
Borrower-ZIP	5 or 9 character zip.
Complete-Letter-Text	self-explanatory
Copy-ID	Unique sequential number assigned to each new copy of any given book when added to the library inventory. Derive the number to assign by scanning "INVENTORY FILE" for numbers already used. Do not reuse numbers. Always assign the next number one greater than the biggest one so far.
Copyright-Date	Copyright data of the book in question.
Date-Requested	Date book was requested to be reserved.
Index-Indic	Does this book have an index?
ISBN	International standard book number.
Publisher	Publisher of the book in question.
Quantity-Ordered	self-explanatory
Reference-City	self-explanatory
Reference-Description	Type of reference (employer, school, teacher, doctor, etc.)
Reference-House	self-explanatory
Reference-Name	self-explanatory
Reference-State	Use standard postal 2-letter codes.
Reference-Street	self-explanatory
Reference-ZIP	5 or 9 character zip.
Subject-Category	Subject (s) of the book in question
Title	Title of the book in question

Table 4-4. Descriptions of data elements

4.2.3 Drawing Material Flow Lines

We will now draw a material flow line to connect the *Borrowers* external to the *Library System* process. The material flow will be named *Borrowed Books* and will look like this:

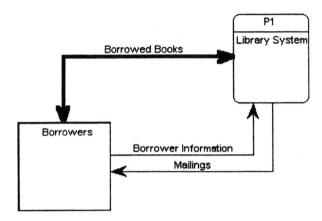

Figure 4-10. Symbols Connected by a Material Flow Line

To draw a material flow line:

1. Pull down the **DFD-GS** menu and select **Material Flow**. Notice the shape of the cursor: a cross next to the pencil. This shape indicates that all lines drawn will be orthogonal (i.e., horizontal and vertical).

2. Place your mouse cursor anywhere within the *Borrowers* symbol. The position of the cursor within the box is irrelevant.

3. Draw the line to the *Library System* process symbol.

Once you release the left mouse button, the **Add Symbol (Data Flow)** dialog appears. Now you can add a name and properties to the data flow.

1. Type the name Borrowed Books in the **Name** box.

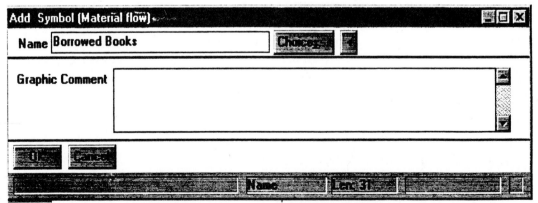

Figure 4-11. Add Symbol dialog

2. Click on **OK**.

3. The definition dialog is displayed, in which are entered the attributes, or data, carried on the data flow line. Enter the data structure name [Books-Checked-Out|Books-Checked-In] the **Data** text box.

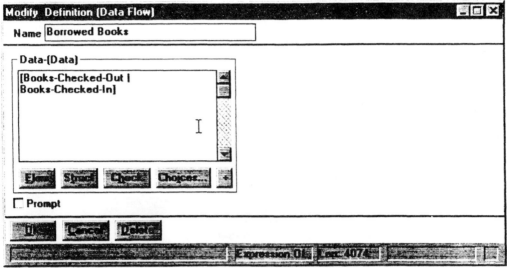

Figure 4-12. Add Definition dialog

4. Select the words *Books-Checked-Out* in the data text box, and click on the **Struct** button at the bottom of the box.

5. The definition dialog is displayed again. Enter the data element name ISBN the **Data** text box.

6. Hit the enter key to move the cursor to the next line.

7. Enter the second data element name, Copy-ID.

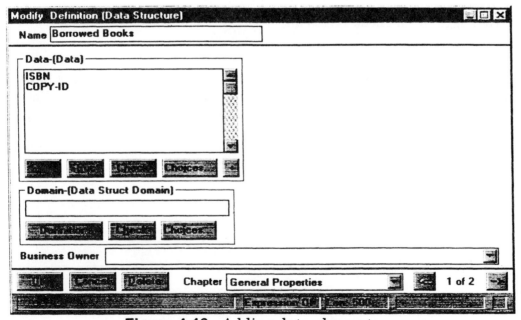

Figure 4-13. Adding data elements

8. Select the word *ISBN* in the data text box, and click on the **Elem** button at the bottom of the box.

9. The **Add Definition (Data Element)** dialog is displayed. Reference *Table 4-4* for the description of *ISBN*. Enter the description in the Description text box, and click on **OK**.

10. Repeat steps 8 and 9 for the second data element, *Copy-ID*.

11. Repeat steps 4 through 10 for the second data structure, *Books-Checked-In*. *Books-Checked-In* contains the same data elements as *Books-Checked-out*.

12. Once the data elements have been defined, select **OK** in the **Add Definition window**.

13. The **Associative Properties** dialog is displayed

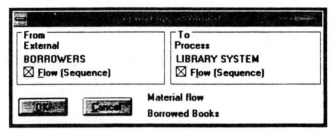

Figure 4-14. The **Associative Property** Dialog

You will notice that the material flow *Borrowed Books* is double-headed. This notation indicates that the same data or material is exchanged in both directions between the external entity and the process. To put the arrowhead on both ends:

13. Toggle both check boxes on.

14. Select **OK**.

15. Repeat the add Material flow process to add the remaining material flow to the diagram. The following table contains the definitions needed to define the flow. Reference *Table 4-4* for the descriptions of each data element.

New Books	data element	ISBN
	data element	Title
	data element	Author-Name
	data element	Publisher
	data element	Copyright-Date
	data element	Bibliography -Indic
	data element	Index-Indic
	data element	Subject-Category

Table 4-5. *New Books* Structure

4.3 Diagram Standards

Most organizations have standards and guidelines for drawing diagrams. Two commonly used standards include:

- The placement of a title descriptive of the diagram at the top of each diagram page. The **Text** command can be used to create titles or other text annotations.

- The inclusion of each diagram name and the date on which it was created or last revised. The **Doc Block** command can be used to place a rectangular symbol containing the diagram name and creation/last modification date. System Architect automatically changes the date and time every time a diagram is modified. The date and time, and other important information can be included as a comment in the Doc Block.

4.3.1 Placing Free-Form Text

The **Text** command is used to add single lines, or multiple-line-blocks, of text to a diagram. Once the text is created, it can be placed on the diagram, moved, and deleted in the same manner as a rectangular symbol. Additionally, text can be enhanced by changing its font type, size, and style.

To place a title on a diagram:

1. Pull down the methodology menu (in this case, **DFD-GS**) and select the **Text** command. The **Add Symbol (Text)** dialog will open.

2. Enter your text, `Library Context Diagram`

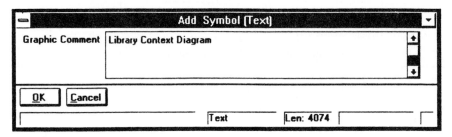

Figure 4-15. The **Add Symbol (Text)** Dialog

3. Click on **OK** once the text has been entered. The **Add Symbol (Text)** dialog will close and the drawing cursor will change to a drawing pencil with an *A* next to it. This indicates System Architect is ready to place your text block.

4. Press and hold down the left mouse button. A dotted rectangle appears in the shape of your entered text. This method is the same used to place any other rectangular symbol.

Figure 4-16. Positioning Free-Form Text

5. While continuing to hold down the mouse button, drag the dotted rectangle into place.

6. Release the mouse button. Your text appears.

4.3.2 Changing the Font Style

To change the font "style" of text which has already been placed:

1. Confirm that you are in the select mode. If you are in the draw mode, or if you are unsure of what mode you are in, click your left mouse button on the *Cursor* button in the toolbox.

2. Select the text by clicking the left mouse button on top of it. The text block will change to reverse video when selected.

3. Pull down the **Set** menu and select the **Font** command. The **Font Style** dialog will open.

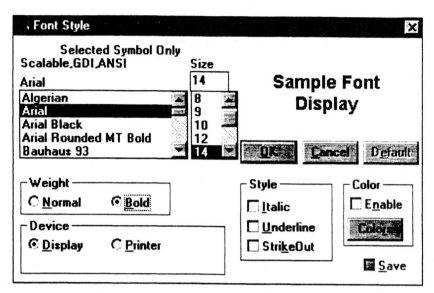

Figure 4-17. The **Font Style** Dialog

4. Select your font name and point size from the scrolling lists and also make your weight and style choices. The effect of each choice is reflected in the sample text window. For this example use the following settings:

   - Font   Arial
   - Point Size   14
   - Weight   Bold

5. Click on **OK**. The text block will change to reflect your font choices.

6. Click anywhere on the diagram in white space to deselect the title.

4.4 Using the Rectangle Tool

This tool can be used to add a free-standing rectangle, or to place a rectangle around text or symbols. To add a rectangle around the free-form text on a drawing:

1. Pull down the methodology menu (**DFD-GS**) and select the **Rectangle** command. Your cursor will change to the familiar pencil-and-rectangle drawing mode shape.

2. Place a rectangle so that it is to the left of the text title and is partially enclosing it.

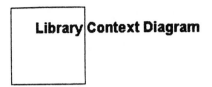

Figure 4-18. Placing a Rectangle

3. Click on the *Cursor* button in the toolbox to change from *draw mode* to *select mode*.

4. Select the rectangle by clicking the mouse inside of it. Handles appear on the corners and sides.

5. Place your cursor on one of the handles and drag the individual sides of the rectangle, thus changing its shape until it encloses the title.

Figure 4-19. Grabbing a Handle to Resize a Rectangle

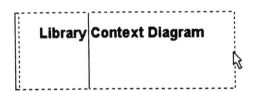

Figure 4-20. Dragging the Side of a Rectangle to Resize It

Figure 4-21. The Resized Rectangle

System Architect: A Guided Tour

☞ *Once a rectangle is placed so it encloses an object, or a block of text, it is not possible to move the rectangle without also moving the objects contained within it. The rectangle can be resized or deleted without affecting the contents, or the individual objects contained within the rectangle can be moved without affecting the rectangle, but the rectangle cannot be moved independently.*

4.5 Adding a Doc Block

Use the **Doc Block** command to add a documentation block to your diagram. This symbol will contain the encyclopedia name of your diagram and the current date and time. It should be placed in a standard place on all diagrams - for example, in the lower right hand corner.

Place the doc block as you would any other rectangular symbol. Also, it can be resized, moved, and deleted just like any other rectangular symbol.
To place a doc block on your diagram, do the following:

1. Pull down the methodology menu (**DFD-GS**).

2. Choose the **Doc Block** command. The drawing cursor changes to the familiar pen-and-rectangle shape indicating drawing mode.

3. Place the doc block as you would any other rectangular symbol.

```
┌─────────────────────────────┐
│    Library Context System    │
│  System Architect Educational │
│    Wed Nov 29, 1995  10:23    │
│────────── Commen ──────────│
│        Joe B. User           │
└─────────────────────────────┘
```

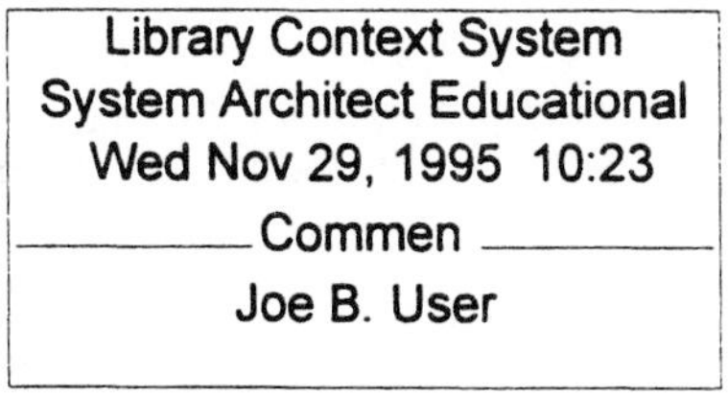

Figure 4-22. The Doc Block

To add a comment to the Doc block:

1. Select the Doc Block by clicking the left mouse button on it.

2. Pull down the **Symbol** menu.

3. Select the **Name, Number, Properties** command.

4. Type in the desired comment; then click the left mouse button on **OK**.

   It may be necessary to resize the Doc Block to display all the text. Refer to *Figures 4-19* and *4-20* for this procedure.

4.6 Printing The Diagram

The **Print** command allows the user to print the current diagram to a specified printer.

To print the *Library Context System* diagram currently displayed in the active window:

1. Pull down the **File** menu and select the **Print** command.

2. The diagram is sent to the printer.

☞ *Please note that the printer options that are changed in System Architect using the **Page Setup** dialog in the **File** menu are not permanent changes to the printer setup. Your printer setup is controlled by Windows.*

4.7 Saving a Diagram

Save your work frequently, using the **Save** command from the **Diagram** menu, or the **Save Diagram** button on the toolbar. Changes to a diagram are not recorded in the encyclopedia until the diagram is saved. Therefore, if you were to lose power to your PC, all the changes you have made to the diagram since opening the diagram (or from your last save) will be lost.

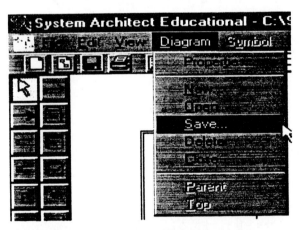

Figure 4-23. The **Diagram** Menu

4.8 Questions in Review

1. List the available line types and their characteristics offered with System Architect.

2. What is the Gane & Sarson diagram notation standard for data flow lines?

3. Assuming the line style is set to straight orthogonal, list two techniques to change the cursor to a "pencil and cross" in order to draw a data flow line.

4. What key would you press to stop drawing a line before you have attached it at both ends to a symbol?

5. List the three ways a data flow arrowhead can be drawn and the meaning of each.

6. What is the difference between a data structure and a data element?

7. What does the notation indicate when a data flow or material flow line is double-headed?

8. What command could be used to place a descriptive title at the top of a data flow diagram?

9. What command could be used to place a rectangular symbol containing the diagram name and the creation/last modification date?

10. What menu and command would you use to add a comment to a Doc Block?

Answers to the above questions can be found in Appendix B.

5. Editing Symbols and Lines

5.1 Moving Symbols

If you accidentally release the mouse button before you move the symbol to the location you want, you can move the misplaced symbol.

1. If the cursor is not the arrow shape, hit the Escape key. So long as the cursor is in the shape of a pencil, it is ready to draw another symbol.

2. Move the cursor point inside the symbol to be moved, and hold down the left mouse button.

3. Keeping the button pressed down, move the mouse until the symbol is in the position you want. Notice that while you're moving the symbol, its normally solid boundaries are replaced by a dotted line.

4. Release the left mouse button.

☞ *If you move the symbol to the boundary of the window, the window automatically scrolls in the direction you are pushing the mouse. This movement can be extremely rapid!*

When in "Select Mode", if a symbol is selected, you cannot move another symbol until the selected one is de-selected. To "de-select" a symbol, either select any other symbol, or move the cursor anywhere outside of a symbol to white space and click the left mouse button.

The process of moving lines is a little different. Please see the next section.

5.2 Modifying Lines

5.2.1 Is The Line Anchored In Place?

In most cases data flow lines are anchored at both ends to symbols. Data flow lines should have an arrowhead on one (or both) ends.

→ If the arrowhead is completely filled in, both ends are attached to another symbol.

→ If the arrowhead is cross-hatched, one end is attached.

→ If the arrowhead is blank, neither end is attached.

5.2.2 Moving Lines

To move an unattached line,

1. Place the cursor anywhere on the line.

2. Holding the left mouse button down, move the line until it is in the desired place. Release the mouse button.

To move an attached line,

1. Select the line by clicking anywhere on the line or the line's name.

2. Grab one of the cross-shaped handles where the line is attached to the other object, and while holding down the left mouse button, move it to the desired location Release the mouse button.

3. Repeat with the other attached end.

To move the anchor point of an attached line,

1. Select it by clicking anywhere on the line or the line's name

2. Grab the cross-shaped handle.

3. Holding the left mouse button down, move the mouse inside the rectangular symbol until the new anchor point is reached. Release the mouse.

5.2.3 Removing Bends from Data Flow Lines

The following steps are used to remove bends from a data flow line which has already been placed.

1. Confirm that you are in the select mode. If you are in the draw mode, or if you are unsure of what mode you are in, click your left mouse button on the *Cursor* button in the toolbox.

2. Select the data flow line by clicking the right mouse button and the **Line** pop-up menu will appear. Also, the line's handles appear, and the name block will be displayed in reverse video.

3. Select the **Reduce Line Segment** command. All bends will now be removed from the line.

5.2.4 Adding Bend Points Into Data Flow Lines

Often a data flow line will be altered, as a process is modified, and a new bend point will be required to route the flow to the new location.

1. Confirm that you are in the select mode. If you are in the draw mode, or if you are unsure of what mode you are in, click your left mouse button on the *Cursor* button in the toolbox.

2. Select the data flow line by clicking the right mouse button and the **Line** pop-up menu will appear. Also, the line's handles appear, and the name block will be displayed in reverse video.

3. Select the **Insert Line Segment** command. The cursor will change to a "pencil and line with 3 handles" shape.

4. Place the cursor in any position along the line and click the left mouse button. A new handle appears; and the cursor will change to a pointer.

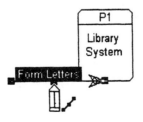

Figure 5-1. Adding a Line Segment

3. Point at the new handle, and press and hold the left mouse button.

4. Drag the new handle to the desired location of the bend.

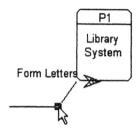

Figure 5-2. Positioning the New Line Segment

5. Release the mouse button; then deselect the line by clicking in white space.

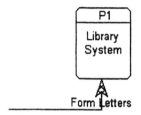

Figure 5-3. The Line After the Segment was Added

5.2.5 Moving Line Names

You may wish to move names to make your diagrams more easily understood. The technique for moving a line name is the same as that for moving a process (or any other diagram object).

To move a name on a line:

1. Place the cursor point inside the name text block, on any of the letters of the name and click the left mouse button to select the name. Press and hold down the mouse button.

2. While holding down the mouse button, drag the name to any new position. Release the mouse button.

3. The line has been automatically selected by this action. Click the mouse button outside of any symbol to deselect it.

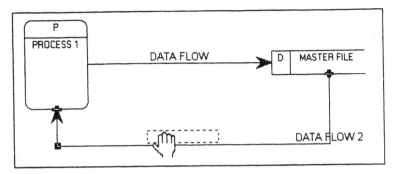

Figure 5-4. Moving the name of a line

☞ *Data flow names will jump back to their original position if the line itself is moved. This is because the* **Auto Reposition Name** *option is toggled* **ON** *in the* **Preferences** *dialog. To prevent data flow names from being moved by System Architect once they have been properly positioned, toggle the* **Auto Reposition Name** *option to* **OFF**.

5.2.6 Reverse Data Flow Direction

1. Select the data flow or material flow.

2. From the **Symbol** Menu, select the **Name, Number, Properties** command.

3. Toggle the appropriate check box(es) on or off. The arrowhead always shows up on the side(s) where the box is toggled on.

☞ *The concept of* input *and* output, *however, is based entirely on the starting point and ending point of the line. The object from which the line started is* always *considered as source; the line is* always *considered output in relation to that object. The arrowheads serve as a graphical representation.*

Therefore, if the real input and output are important, it may be prudent to delete an erroneously directed line, and redraw it.

5.3 Removing Unintentionally Placed Symbols

There are three ways to remove an unwanted symbol.

Method 1. Press the "Delete Last Symbol key", F9.

Pressing the F9 key deletes the last placed symbol on a diagram.

☞ *The F9 key does not work as an "undo/redo" key. The F9 key only removes the last-placed symbol on a diagram.*

Method 2. Select the unwanted symbol and press the Delete key.

Method 3. Select the unwanted symbol, pull down the **Edit** menu and select the **Delete** command.

☞ *If you cannot remember which symbol you placed last, use the F10 key. This key is also useful if your diagram is crowded and you are having difficulty selecting a particular symbol. The F10 key will select symbols in the order in which they were placed on the diagram. Once you have selected the unwanted symbol, use Method 2 or 3 to remove it.*

5.4 Modifying Definitions

During the process of analysis and design, more information is discovered about the objects to be used in the new system. Since analysis is iterative, it is common to go back and modify existing definitions. To modify any of the definitions in your encyclopedia:

- If the diagram is open, double-click on the symbol to be modified, or

- From the **Definition** Menu, select **Modify**. Select the type of the object to be modified (process, data flow, data store, etc.), or enter the name of the specific object. Click on the *Search* button to display a list of objects that match the criteria.

5.5 Numbering Processes and/or Data Stores

The Gane & Sarson and Yourdon/DeMarco methodologies prefer that processes and data stores be numbered. To make sure the symbols in your data flows are numbered consecutively, **Auto Number** must be toggled on in the Preferences Dialog.

If, however, you started drawing with **Auto Number** toggled off, make corrections as follows:

1. Select one process symbol from your drawing.

2. From the **Symbol** Menu, select the **Name, Number, Properties** command.

3. Input the correct number in the **Number** text box and click **OK**.

5.6 Using Pop-Up Menus

Three types of pop-up menus are available in System Architect: one for diagram commands, one for rectangular symbol commands, and one for line symbol commands. Most of the commands included in the pop-up menus are available from pull down menus.

The pop-up menu for a diagram is opened by clicking the right mouse button on white space. Note that the **Parent** and **Top** commands will only be included in the pop-up menu for a diagram that is the child of a symbol contained on another diagram; similarly, they are grayed in the **Diagram** menu unless the current diagram is a child diagram.

Figure 5-5. The **Diagram** Pop-Up Menu

The pop-up menu for a rectangular symbol is opened by clicking the right mouse button on the symbol; the symbol will be selected and the menu will be opened at the same time.

Note that the **Child Create** and **Child Attach** commands will only be included in the pop-up menu for a symbol that has not yet been expanded to a child diagram, while the **Child Detach** and **Child Open** commands will only be included in the pop-up menu for a symbol that has been expanded to a child diagram.

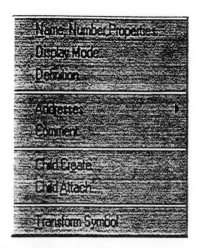

Figure 5-6. The **Rectangular Symbol** Pop-Up Menu

The pop-up menu for a line symbol is opened by clicking your right mouse button on the symbol; the symbol will be selected, and the menu will be opened at the same time.

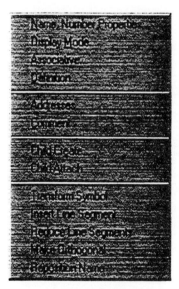

Figure 5-7. The **Line Symbol** Pop-Up Menu

5.7 Questions in Review

1. When in "Select Mode", what shape is the cursor in order to move a symbol?

2. List two methods to "de-select" a symbol.

3. List the procedure for removing bends from a data flow line.

4. What shape will the cursor change to when selecting the **Insert Line Segment** command?

5. If a data flow name has been properly positioned, what must you do to prevent the name from being moved by System Architect when the data flow line is repositioned.

6. List the three methods for removing an unwanted symbol.

7. What function does the F10 key serve?

8. What must you do to ensure the symbols in your data flow diagrams are numbered consecutively?

9. List the three types of pop-up menus available in System Architect.

10. Under what condition will the commands **Child Create** and **Child Attach** be included in the pop-up menu for a symbol?

Answers to the above questions can be found in Appendix B.

6. Creating A Child Diagram

In this chapter we are going to create a child data flow diagram of the Library
System process shown in *Figure 6-1*.

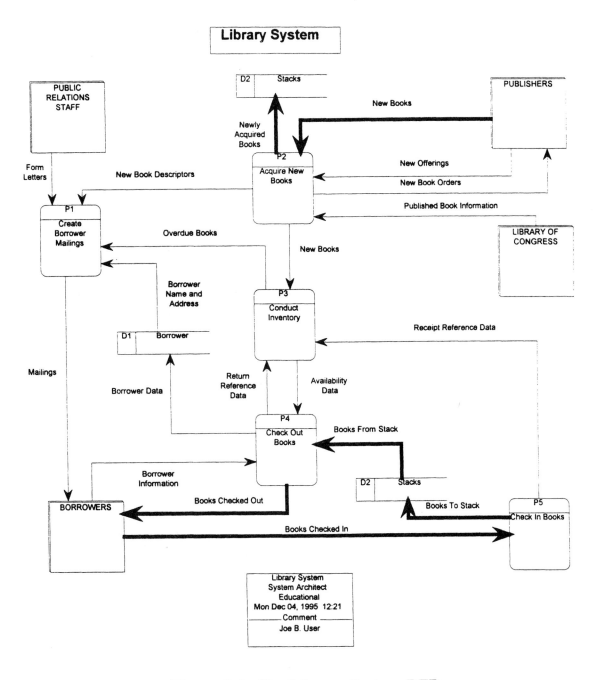

Figure 6-1. The Library System DFD

6.1 Opening The Parent Diagram

This section assumes you have started System Architect and opened the *Project1* encyclopedia. If you haven't, please do so at this time.

1. Pull down the **Diagram** menu and click **Open**. The **Select For Opening** dialog will be displayed. Click **Search**.

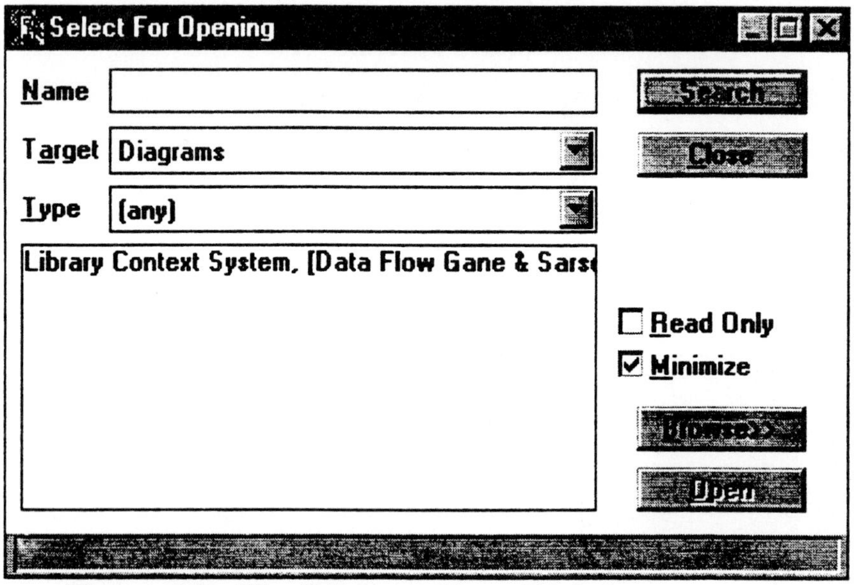

Figure 6-2. The Diagram Open Dialog

2. System Architect will search for all diagrams of any type and list them in the text box. Select the *Library Context System* diagram and click **Open**.

The Library Context System diagram is displayed.

6.2 Parent - Child Relationship

The ability to have "parent" and "child" diagrams is critical to the success of any Structured Analysis project. The diagram containing the parent symbol remains relatively simple, while a child diagram is used to display an extra level of complexity. If the child diagram becomes too complex, an even lower level set of child diagrams can be created. In theory, there is no limit to the number of levels that can be created, but in practice it is best not to exceed 4 or 5. The process of creating parent and child data flow diagrams (DFD's) is known as *leveling*, with the result being a *set of leveled* DFD's

"Leveling" can be defined through the following four statements:

- The diagram contains a given process symbol, the parent process, in which the complexity of the process is hidden.

- The parent process symbol is expanded into an entire child diagram that is used to explain the hidden complexity of the process.

- Therefore, the parent process and the child diagram are equivalent.

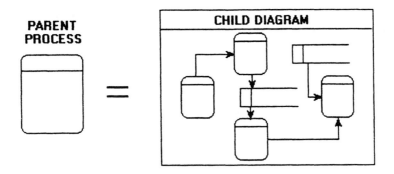

Figure 6.3. Parent Process = Child Diagram

- This is a logical equivalence; therefore, any data flowing into the parent process symbol must also flow into the child diagram. Similarly, any data flowing out of the parent process symbol must also flow out of the child diagram.

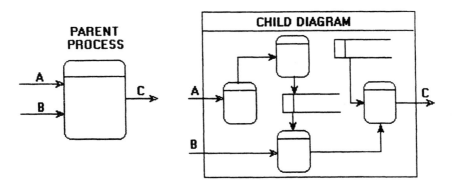

Figure 6.4. Data into Parent Process = Data into Child Diagram

6.3 Specifying Level Numbers

Decimal point numbering is the standard way to identify process symbols, with an additional decimal point being added each time a new child level is created. Below, you can see how Process "P1" has a child diagram with processes numbered P1.1, P1.2, etc.

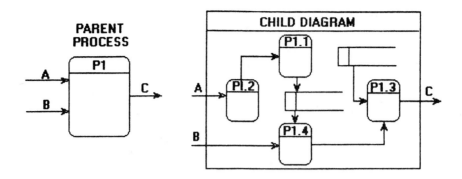

Figure 6.5. Level Number Specifications

Numbers are assigned to processes arbitrarily. This means that P1.1 should not be considered more important than P1.2, or that its processing occurs sooner. If process P1.3 requires expansion into the next level of child diagram, processes on that child will be P1.3.1, P1.3.2, P1.3.3, etc.

Before proceeding with the creation of a child diagram, it is important to verify that the correct options have been set to allow for level numbering of the processes that will be created. The settings must be set on both the global level and the symbol level.

To set Global Level options:

1. Pull down the **Set** menu and choose the **Preferences** command.

2. Verify that the **Auto Number** option is set to **ON**.

3. Click on **OK**.

6.4 Creating the Child Diagram

This diagram will show the major functional components of the Library System. It is often called the Level 1 or System Level diagram.

To begin the creation of a child diagram:

1. Select the process symbol in the context diagram which will be equivalent to the child (Library System).

2. Pull down the **Symbol** menu.

3. Click on **Child**.

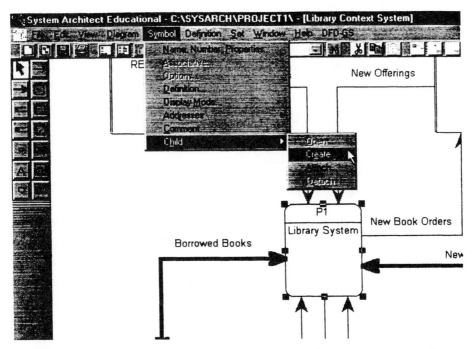

Figure 6.6 The **Symbol** Menu, **Child Create** command

4. Choose the **Create** command. System Architect will display the
    Create Child dialog, which is essentially the same as the **New
    Diagram** dialog. The difference between the two dialogs is that the
    Child Create dialog provides a default diagram type, that is the same
    as the diagram containing the parent symbol, and a default diagram
    name, that is the same as the parent symbol.

    You may change the name or diagram type by simply selecting
    something else.

    To accept the selections, click on **OK**.

Figure 6.7 The **Child Create** Dialog

Notice that in the **Child Create** dialog, the **Name** field is already filled in with the name of the parent process. This standard is considered to be a good one to follow - since the child diagram and the parent process are one and the same, only the level of detail has changed. The parent process has been moved under a magnifying glass, so to speak.

☞   *It is possible to change the name and type of diagram at this point. This flexibility could be useful if, for instance, you wanted to level a data flow or data store to an entity relationship model.*

---

5. System Architect will prompt you to save changes to the diagram containing the parent symbol. Click on **Yes**.

You must answer **Yes**, even if you have not made any changes to the diagram since it was last saved. During the process of creating a child diagram, System Architect adds notation at the parent symbol to signify that a diagram has been created to expand the symbol. System Architect is essentially asking to save the notation it has added to your diagram; it will not permit you to create a child diagram if you do not save the diagram that it has altered.

6. Once the diagram containing the parent symbol has been saved, you will be presented with the **Leveling Data** dialog, used to specify what material should be placed on the child diagram. This dialog contains three check boxes: **Image of Parent Symbol, Lines/Flows Attached to Parent**, and **Symbols Attached to Lines/Flows**.

Toggle off the **Image of Parent Symbol** selection, then click on **OK**.

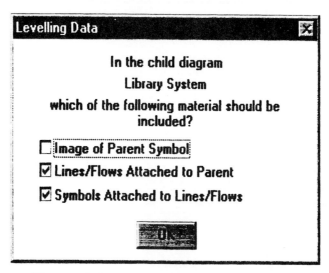

Figure 6.8. The **Leveling Data** dialog

You are now looking at a new diagram, but it is not empty. System Architect has placed flow lines and "uncle" symbols, as specified in the Leveling Data dialog.

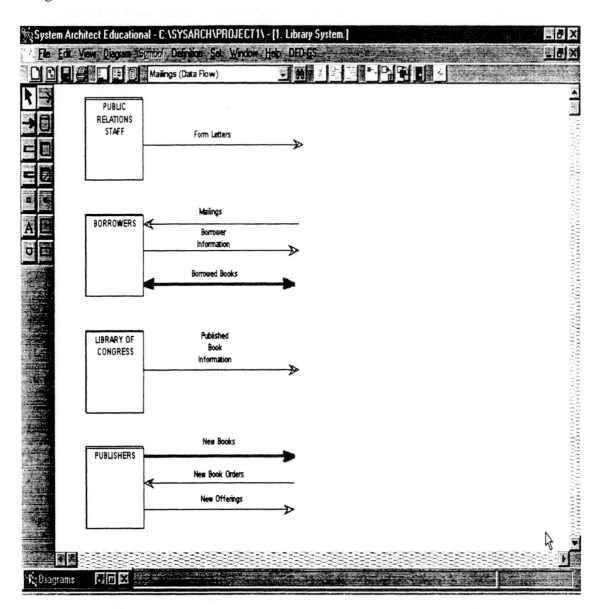

Figure 6.9. Creating the Library System Child Diagram

☞   *System Architect supports the use of multiple windows. The new child diagram appears in a separate window. In this way, you can arrange both the parent diagram and child diagram on your screen.*

6.5 Completing Your Level 1 Diagram

The "Uncle" symbols, and attached input and output data flows can be moved to their respective positions on the diagram. The necessary process and data store symbols can then be placed in their proper positions in the center, and the input and output flows can then be connected to the correct process symbols.

1. Move the Entity symbols to their respective position as shown in *Figure 6-1* in preparation for adding the process and data store symbols.

6.5.1 Adding The Child Processes

1. Pull down the **DFD-GS** menu and select *Process*, or select the Process symbol from the Toolbox.

   The cursor changes to a "pencil and rectangle." The pencil indicates you are in "draw" mode, ready to place symbols in your diagram. The rectangle tells you that you will be placing a rectangular shaped symbol; a process symbol in this case.

2. Move the cursor into the drawing space and press on the left mouse button. A process symbol appears above and to the left of the cursor. Move the process to the location of *P1.1, Create Borrower Mailings*, as shown in *Figure 6-1*.

3. The **Add Symbol (Process)** dialog box is displayed since the **Auto Name** option is set on in the **Preferences** dialog. Type Create Borrower Mailings in the **Name** text box.

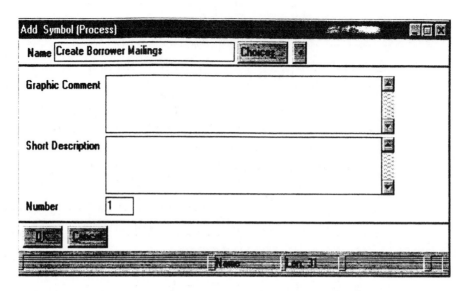

Figure 6-10. Enter the name in the **Add Symbol [Process]** Dialog Box

5. Click on **OK**.

6. The **Add Definition (Process)** dialog is displayed. Click **OK**.

7. Repeat Steps 1 through 6 above to add the remaining processes:

    *   Acquire New Books

    *   Conduct Inventory

    *   Check Out Books

    *   Check In Books

6.5.2 Adding The Data Stores

1. Pull down the **DFD-GS** menu and select **Data Store**, or select the Data Store symbol from the Toolbox.

2. Move the cursor into the drawing space and press on the left mouse button. A data store symbol appears above and to the left of the cursor. Move the data store to the location of *D1, Borrower File,* as shown in *Figure 6-1.*

3. The **Add Symbol (Data Store)** dialog box is displayed since the **Auto Name** option is set on in the **Preferences** dialog. Type Borrower in the **Name** text box.

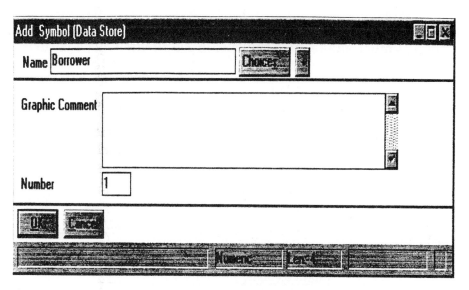

Figure 6-11. Enter the name in the **Add Symbol [Data Store]** Dialog Box

4. Be sure the **Number** is specified as 1. Click on **OK**.

5. The **Add Definition (Data Store)** dialog is displayed. Enter the data elements as shown in *Figure 6-12*.

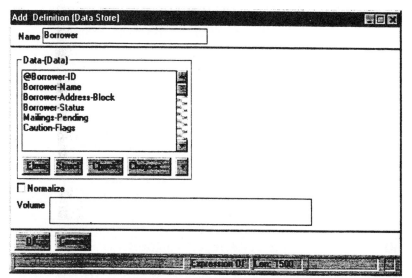

Figure 6-12. The **Add Definition [Data Store]** Dialog Box

6. Define each of the data elements by selecting its name and clicking Elem or Struct. This procedure was introduced in *Chapter 4* if you need to review. The definitions of the data structures and data elements can be found in *Tables 6-1, 6-3 and 6-4*.

7. Once all data elements have been defined Click **OK**.

8. Repeat Steps 1 through 6 above to add the remaining data store, STACKS, with its data element listed in table 6-1.

Notice in *Figure 6-1* the data store *Stacks* is duplicated. To be able to duplicate a symbol, make sure the option *Duplicate Check* is turned off.

Data Store	Contains	
STACKS	data element	"No Definition Required"

Table 6-1. Data Store Data Elements

Data Flow	Contains	
AVAILABILITY DATA	data element	Copy-ID
	data element	Current-Copy-Location
	data element	Owning-Branch-ID
BOOKS FROM STACK	data element	@ISBN
	data element	Copies-Borrowed
	data element	Branch-ID
BOOKS TO STACK	data element	@ISBN
	data element	Copies-Borrowed
	data element	Branch-ID
BORROWER DATA	data element	Borrower-ID
	data structure	Borrower-Name
	data structure	Borrower-Address-Block
	data structure	Caution-Flags
BORROWER NAME AND ADDRESS	data element	Borrower-ID
	data structure	Borrower-Name
	data structure	Borrower-Address-Block
MAILINGS	data-element	Complete-Letter-Text
	data structure	Borrower-Name
	data structure	Borrower-Address-Block
NEW BOOK DESCRIPTORS	data element	@ISBN
	data element	Title
	data element	Author-Name
	data element	Copyright-Date
	data element	Publisher
	data element	Subject-Category
NEW BOOKS	data element	"New Books"
NEWLY ACQUIRED BOOKS	data element	"New Books"
OVERDUE BOOKS	data element	@ISBN
	data element	Copy-ID
	data element	Borrower-ID
	data element	Date-Borrowed
	data element	Days-May-Keep
RECEIPT REFERENCE DATA	data element	Date-Returned
	data element	Owning-Branch-ID
	data element	Copy-ID
RETURN REFERENCE DATA	data element	Owning-Branch-ID
	data element	Copy-ID
	data element	Borrower-ID
	data element	Date-Borrowed
	data element	Days-May-Keep

Table 6-2. Data Flow Data Elements

Data Structure Name	Component Data
Borrower-Address-Block	Borrower-House
	Borrower-Street
	Borrower-City
	Borrower-State
	Borrower-ZIP
Borrower-Name	Borrower-Last-Name
	Borrower-First-Name
	Borrower-Middle-Init
Caution-Flags	Caution-Chronic-Overdues
	Caution-Suspected-Thief
	Caution-Known-Thief
	Caution-Suspected-Vandal
	Caution-Known-Vandal

Table 6-3. Data Structure Data Elements

Data Element	Description
Author-Name	Author of book
Bibliography-Indic	Does this book have a bibliography?
Borrower-City	self-explanatory
Borrower-First-Name	self-explanatory
Borrower-House	Borrower house number.
Borrower-ID	If possible, user borrower's SSN else use the next available ID.
Borrower-Last-Name	self-explanatory
Borrower-Middle-Init	self-explanatory
Borrower-State	Use standard postal 2-letter codes.
Borrower-Status	0=active, 1=applicant, 2=inactive
Borrower-Street	self-explanatory
Borrower-ZIP	5 or 9 character zip.
Caution-Chronic-Overdues	5 or more overdues in prior 12 months
Caution-Known-Thief	self-explanatory
Caution-Known-Vandal	self-explanatory
Caution-Suspected-Thief	self-explanatory
Caution-Suspected-Vandal	self-explanatory
Complete-Letter-Text	self-explanatory
Copies-Being-Repaired	Number of copies of this book currently at bindery for repair.
Copies-Borrowed	Number of copies of this book in hands of borrowers.
Copies-In-Stacks	Number of copies of this book available for lending.

Data Element	Description
Copies-On-Order	Number of copies of this book back-ordered from publisher.
Copies-Owned	Number of copies of this book owned by the library system as of 10/04/95.
Copy-ID	Unique sequential number assigned to each new copy of any given book when added to the library inventory. Derive the number to assign by scanning "INVENTORY FILE" for numbers already used. Do not reuse numbers. Always assign the next number one greater than the biggest one so far.
Copyright-Date	Copyright data of the book in question.
Current-Copy-Location	Location of the book in question. Valid choices are: 1. In the stacks of Main or one of the 5 branches 2. Borrowed by "Borrower-ID" 3. At the BINDERY for repair
Date-Borrowed	self-explanatory
Date-Card-Expires	self-explanatory
Date-Letter-Sent	self-explanatory
Date-Requested	Date user asked a book to be reserved for them.
Days-May-Keep	Usually 14 days, but may differ for certain reference books. Date is stamped inside the cover.
Inactive-Date	Date borrower became inactive.
Index-Indic	Does this book have an index?
ISBN	International standard book number.
Mailings-Pending	Y/N
New Books	self-explanatory
Owning-Branch-ID	Branch book in question was assigned to. Borrower may return any book to any branch, but every attempt should be made to return a book back to its owning branch.
Publisher	Publisher of the book in question.
Reference-City	self-explanatory
Reference-Description	Type of reference (employer, school, teacher, doctor, etc.)
Reference-House	self-explanatory
Reference-Name	self-explanatory
Reference-State	Use standard postal 2-letter codes.
Reference-Street	self-explanatory
Reference-ZIP	5 or 9 character zip.
Status	None
Subject-Category	Subject (s) of the book in question

Data Element	Description
Title	Title of the book in question

Table 6-3. Descriptions of Data Elements

6.6 Attaching a Data Flow Line

Once the symbols have been placed, the data flow lines must be attached to the process. This task is performed in three steps:

1. Pull down the **Set** menu and choose the **Preferences** command. Make sure that the **Auto Reposition Name** option is set to **ON** in the **Preferences** dialog, else the name may not be moved with the flow line.

2. Select the flow to be moved. For an input flow, place the cursor in the handle at the arrow head; for an output flow, use the handle at the tail.

3. Press and hold the left mouse button while dragging the handle up against the symbol's border. It is a good idea to move the cursor slightly inside the symbol (the handle will remain outside), then release the button.

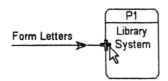

Figure 6-13. Attaching Data Flow Lines

The arrow head will change from a cross-hatched pattern to being completed filled in, signifying that the arrow has indeed been attached to the process symbol.

The creation of child diagrams, and attachment of pre-existing data flow lines, is a common situation which requires the addition of line segments. First the data flow line must be attached; then additional bends can be added into the line as discussed in *Chapter 5*.

6.6.1 Creating Multi-Line Data Flow Names

It may be necessary to create multi-line data flow names to make your diagram more readable. The following procedure will change a single line data flow name into a two line data flow name.

1. To edit a data flow line name so that it appears on multiple lines:

   - Select the name to be changed.

   - Pull down the **Symbol** menu and click **Name, Number, Properties**.

   - Click in the **+** button to expand the Name field.

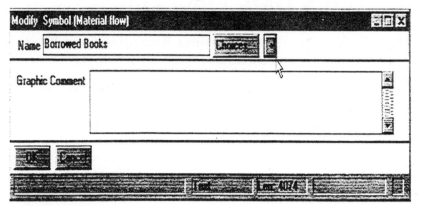

Figure 6-14. Placing a Two-Line Data Flow Name

   - Enter a carriage return where you would like to end the first line.

   - Type the remainder of the name onto the next line in the dialog box.

The second line of text will be placed under the first on the diagram.

☞   *A blank character must be placed at the end of each line before the carriage return. Otherwise, System Architect will not register the blank characters in the process names; i.e., it will read* Check Out Books *as* CheckOutBooks. *There may be level balancing problems later.*

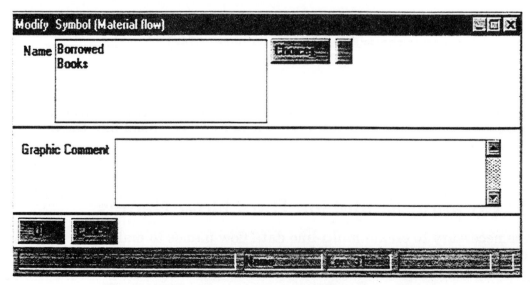

Figure 6-15. Placing a Two-Line Data Flow Name

6.7 Drawing The Remaining Diagram Lines

6.7.1 Drawing The Remaining Data Flow Lines

Once all the existing data flows have been attached, we need to add the
additional data flows pictured in Figure 6-1.

1. Pull down the **DFD-GS** menu and select the **Data Flow** command
    or select the line symbol from the Toolbox.

    Draw the following data flow lines. Reference *Chapter 4* for a review of
    the procedure if necessary.

      - Mailings
      - New Book Descriptors
      - Overdue Books
      - Borrower Name and Address
      - Borrower Data
      - Receipt Reference Data
      - Return Reference Data
      - Availability Data

    Reference *Tables 6-2, 6-3, and 6-4* for the data element definitions.

6.7.2 Drawing The Remaining Material Flow Lines

It is now time to draw the remaining material flows pictured in *Figure 6-1*.

1. Pull down the **DFD-GS** menu and select **Material Flow**.

Draw the following material flow lines. Reference *Chapter 4* for a review of the procedure if necessary.

- Books From Stack
- Books To Stack
- Newly Acquired Books
- Books Checked Out
- Books Checked In

Reference Tables 6-2, 6-3, and 6-4 for the data element definitions.

Note that the material flow called *Borrowed Books* on the Library Context Diagram is equivalent to the sum of *Books Checked In* and *Books Checked Out* on the Library System Diagram.

2. Delete the material flow Borrowed Books.

6.8 Adding A Diagram Title and Doc Block

6.8.1 Adding A Diagram Title

To add the diagram title:

1. Select the *Text* symbol from the Toolbox.

2. Enter the diagram name Library System in the **Add Symbol (Text)** dialog. Click on **OK**.

3. Text appears as a rectangular dotted line. Move it to the center of the diagram, at the top. Note that it is still selected after you place it.

4. Do not de-select the title. From the **Set** Menu, select the **Font** command.

5. Select the type face and size you want from the *Font Style* dialog. Select any other attributes you think are appropriate for a title: bold, italic, underline, and so on. Click on **OK**.

6.8.2 Adding A Doc Block

To add the Doc (short for Documentation) Block:

1. ▨ Select the *Doc Block* symbol from the Toolbox.

2. Drop it in the lower center of the diagram, below the *Books Checked In* material flow.

3. The Doc Block does not have a name or a definition. To enter any extra comments, put the cursor inside the symbol, and click with the right mouse button.

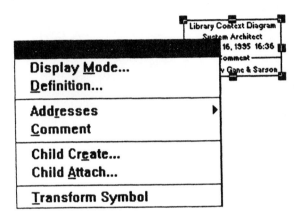

Figure 6-16. The floating menu

4. Select the *Name, Number, Properties* command.

5. Enter any appropriate comments, such as your name then click **OK**.

6.9 Printing The Diagram

The **Print** command allows the user to print the current diagram to a specified printer.

To print the *Library Context System* diagram currently displayed in the active window:

1. Pull down the **File** menu and select the **Print** command.

2. The diagram is sent to the printer.

☞ *Please note that the printer options that are changed in System Architect using the **Setup** dialog in the **File** menu **Print** option are not permanent changes to the printer setup. Your printer setup is controlled by Windows.*

6.10 Saving a Diagram

Save your work frequently, using the **Save** command from the **Diagram** menu, or the **Save Diagram** button on the toolbar. Changes to a diagram are not recorded in the encyclopedia until the diagram is saved. Therefore, if you were to lose power to your PC, all the work you have done since opening the diagram (or from your last save) will be lost.

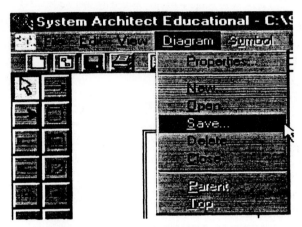

Figure 6-17. The **Diagram** Menu

6.10 Questions in Review

1. Define "leveling".

2. How would System Architect number three processes in a child diagram, if the process in the parent diagram was numbered P1?

3. In the **Child Create** dialog, the **Name** field is already filled in with the name of the parent process. Why is this a good standard to follow?

4. When creating a child diagram, System Architect presents you with a dialog box containing three choices of material to placed on the child diagram. What are the three choices of material?

5. What is an "uncle" symbol?

6. Does System Architect support the use of multiple windows? Why would use multiple windows?

7. What is the fill pattern of the arrowhead of a data flow line that is properly attached to symbols at both ends?

8. To place duplicate symbols in a diagram what option must be turned off?

9. List the procedure for converting a one-line data flow name into a two-line data flow name?

10. When creating a multi-line data flow name, why must you place a blank character at the end of the line before the carriage return?

Answers to the above questions can be found in Appendix B.

7. Running Process Modeling Reports

The System Architect Reporting System allows the user to specify queries and reports using information stored in the project dictionary. System Architect provides over one hundred pre-written reports that cover a wide range of project reporting requirements.

7.1 Running a report

The purpose of this section is to demonstrate how the pre-written reports are run. These reports are included on the System Architect program diskette that you received with the product at the time of purchase. If the recommended installation was followed, the reports will be found in the REPORTS.RPT file contained in the same directory as the System Architect executable module, usually C:\SYSARCH.

This section assumes you have started System Architect and opened the *Project1* encyclopedia. If you haven't, please do so at this time.

The following procedure is used to run a report to produce a listing of diagrams within the *Project1* encyclopedia.

1. Pull down the **File** menu, and select the **Reports** command. System Architect will take a minute to load the default report files; a selection box will then appear containing a list of available reports contained in the selected reports file.

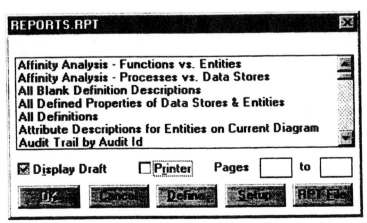

Figure 7-1. Selecting a Report form the REPORTS.RPT File

For this manual we are using the REPORTS.RPT file; the file may be changed by clicking on the **RPT File** button, located on the lower right hand corner of the **Reports** dialog, and selecting a new file.

2. Select the report named *Diagram Listing by Name* by scrolling the dialog box to its location and clicking the left mouse button on it.

3. Since we will not be printing the report now, click the left mouse button once in the **Printer** check box; it will become empty.   The printer box is a three-phase control box; it will either be empty, contain an X or check-mark, or be grayed. The report will not be sent to the printer if the box is empty. The report will always be printed if the box contains an X or check-mark, and the default print settings will be used if the box is grayed.

4. Select the **Display Draft** check box to place an X or check-mark in it. The output will be displayed in draft format on your screen.

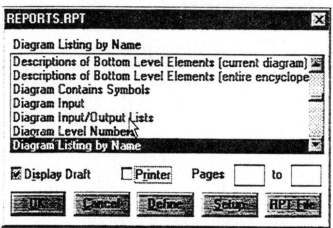

Figure 7-2.   The **REPORTS.RPT** Dialog Window

5. Click on **OK** to run the report

The resulting "draft" report may look something like the following:

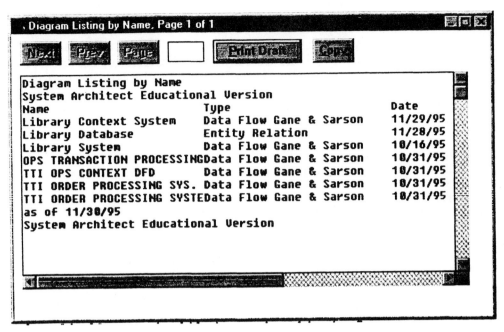

Figure 7-2. The Draft Output for a Report

     6. Close the report window.

Formatting, such as bold text, only appears when the output is routed directly to the printer. It will not be shown on this display. A draft report can be composed much quicker than a fully-formatted printout. Font commands, such as *bold* or *italic* are ignored when creating a draft report. Format commands, such as *width*, and graphics commands, such as *underline* or *draw borders*, are also ignored.

7.2 Locating the Correct Pre-written Report

Over one-hundred reports are available to choose from in the selection box; therefore, it may be difficult to locate the report that will meet specific requirements.

     1. The reports are listed in the **Reports** dialog in alphabetical order by report name. To quickly scroll to a report that is not in the initial window, select any report and press the keyboard key corresponding to the first letter of the report title to be retrieved. The first report title starting with that letter will be scrolled to and selected. Repeat pressing the same letter key until the desired report is visible, or use the slide bar located on the right side of the title window.

7.3 System Architect Rule-Checking Reports

System Architect provides a comprehensive set of rule-checking reports for examining the quality of both process and data models. These rule-checking programs look at the diagrams, read the dictionary definitions of all the symbols, and apply quality tests to the work. The specific tests are based on the following criteria:

System models must be:

- *Complete* - All diagram symbols must be defined and all necessary non-symbol definitions, such as data elements, must exist.

- *Correct* - Each methodology contains rules, or diagram notation, for drawing diagrams. System Architect will examine the diagram and dictionary entries to verify adherence to the rules. For example, each process on data flow diagrams must have at least one input data flow and one output data flow.

- *Consistent* - Consistency is measured in two dimensions:

  1. An individual diagram must be consistent within itself: For example, a data store definition must include all data elements that are specified on the combination of input and output data flows to that data store.

  2. A diagram must be consistent with other related diagrams in the model. For example, each "child diagram" must "balance" to its "parent symbol"; all the data entering a parent process and leaving it must also be represented on its attached child diagram.

7.3.1 Rule-Checking Programs

Rule-checking programs applicable to process modeling will be run in the following section. These programs include:

1. The *Rules Check* report which applies the rules of data flow diagrams to the process model diagrams. For example, this report will examine each diagram to verify that all process symbols have at least one attached input data flow and at least one attached output data flow.

2. The *Balance Children* report checks that a selected parent symbol is consistent with its related child diagram.

3. The *Balance Parent* report applies the same rule-checks as the *Balance Children* report. The difference is that *Balance Parent* starts the comparison from the child diagram in the active window.

4. The *Balance Horizontal* report verifies that data store definitions include all the data elements. This includes elements posted and retrieved from the data store on attached data flows. This report also checks all elements defined on data flows that enter and leave AND and OR connectors.

5. The *Expression Check* report checks for correct expression statement syntax in dictionary definitions of data stores and data flows.

7.3.2 Running Rule-Checking Reports

Errors and inconsistencies can creep into the design during the months that a project team spends capturing the voluminous details of a new system. Specifically, errors concerning processing and data structures in the encyclopedia are introduced. System Architect provides a comprehensive set of rule-checking programs to assist in locating and eliminating problems. The rule-checking programs examine the diagrams, read the dictionary definitions of symbols contained in the diagram, and apply quality tests to the work. The tests check that the system models and definitions are complete, correct, and consistent.

Three rule-checking reports will be run using the parent and child diagrams created in Chapter 4 and chapter 6.

The more in-depth reports test for adherence to methodology-based rules, internal consistency within diagrams, and consistency with related diagrams. The rule-checking reports are in the REPORTS.RPT file. These reports can also be run from the methodology menu by selecting the report type from the **DFD-GS** menu.

7.3.2.1 Rules Check Report

The *Rules Check* report is often the first rule-checking report to be run. This report checks for violations of data flow diagram conventions. For example, each process must have at least one input data flow and one output data flow. If not, the process is called a *miracle* or *black hole*.

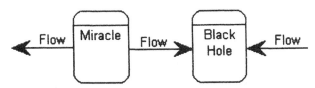

Figure 7-3.   Miracles and Black Holes

The *Rules Check* report is run from the methodology menu.

1. Open the *Library Context Diagram*.

2. Pull down the **DFD-GS** menu and select the **Rules Check** command.

System Architect will check the current diagram for violations. If violations
were found, it displays the results in a report. The report may be printed or
viewed on-line, in order to assist you in correcting the violations.

If violations were discovered, System Architect places error marks on the
diagram where the violation occurred.

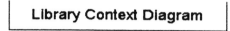

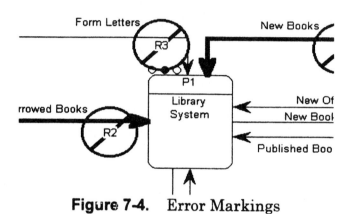

Figure 7-4.   Error Markings

To remove the error markings from the diagram:

   1. Pull down the **DFD-GS** menu and select the **Clear Errors** command.

Once the error markings are removed, the diagram can be modified to correct
the noted violations and the report can be re-run. If no violations are detected
when the report is executed, a message window indicating the report is empty
will be displayed.

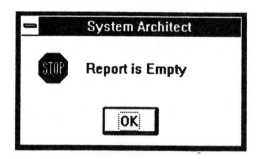

Figure 7-5. The **Report is Empty** Message

7.3.2.2 Level Balancing Reports

The *Balance Child(ren)* and *Balance Parent* reports check that one diagram is
consistent with another related diagram in the model. For example, each *child*

diagram must balance to its *parent symbol.* That is, all the data elements entering a parent process and leaving it, must also be represented on its attached child diagram. If not, the parent symbol and child diagram do not represent the same input-process/output activity.

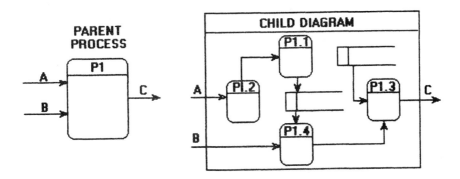

Figure 7-6. Balancing the Parent Process with the Child Diagram

To run the *Balance Children* report:

1. Select the *Library System* process symbol of the *Library Context Diagram.*

2. Pull down the **DFD-GS** menu and select the **Balance Child(ren)** command.

3. Answer **No** to the "Save changes to diagram ---" dialog.

4. The *Balance Children report* is displayed.

5. Note any violations that need to be corrected.

To run the *Balance Parent* report:

1. Open the child diagram *Library System.*

2. Pull down the **DFD-GS** menu and select the **Balance Parent** command.

3. Answer **No** to the "Save changes to diagram ---" dialog.

4. The *Balance Parent report* is displayed.

5. Note any violations that need to be corrected.

Be sure to save your corrected diagrams and then exit System Architect.

7.4 Questions in Review

1. What is the name of the file that System Architect defaults to, which contains over 100 pre-written reports?

2. Name the differences between printing a draft report and printing a fully formatted report.

3. What three criteria are rules checking reports based on?

4. Name four process modeling rule checking programs.

5. Which rule-checking report is usually the first to be run and checks for violations of data flow diagram conventions?

6. What is it called if a process does not have at least one input data flow and one output data flow?

7. If when running a rule checking report violations are discovered, what happens to your diagram?

8. What is the procedure to remove the error markings from a diagram.

9. Define the *Balance Children* report.

10. List the procedure for running the *Balance Parent* report.

Answers to the above questions can be found in Appendix B.

8. Data Modeling with ERDs

Data flow diagrams (DFD's) are the standard notation for recording the data
that moves through a system, including how it is acted on, stored, and retrieved.
The *Process Model* is comprised of a leveled set of DFD's.

Entity Relation Diagrams (ERD's) display the entities (or things) of interest to
the organization, data (information) that comprises the entities from the
business perspective, and the relationships between the entities.

In this chapter of the manual we will begin creating the Library System data
model as shown in *Figure 8-1* and finish it in *Chapter 9*.

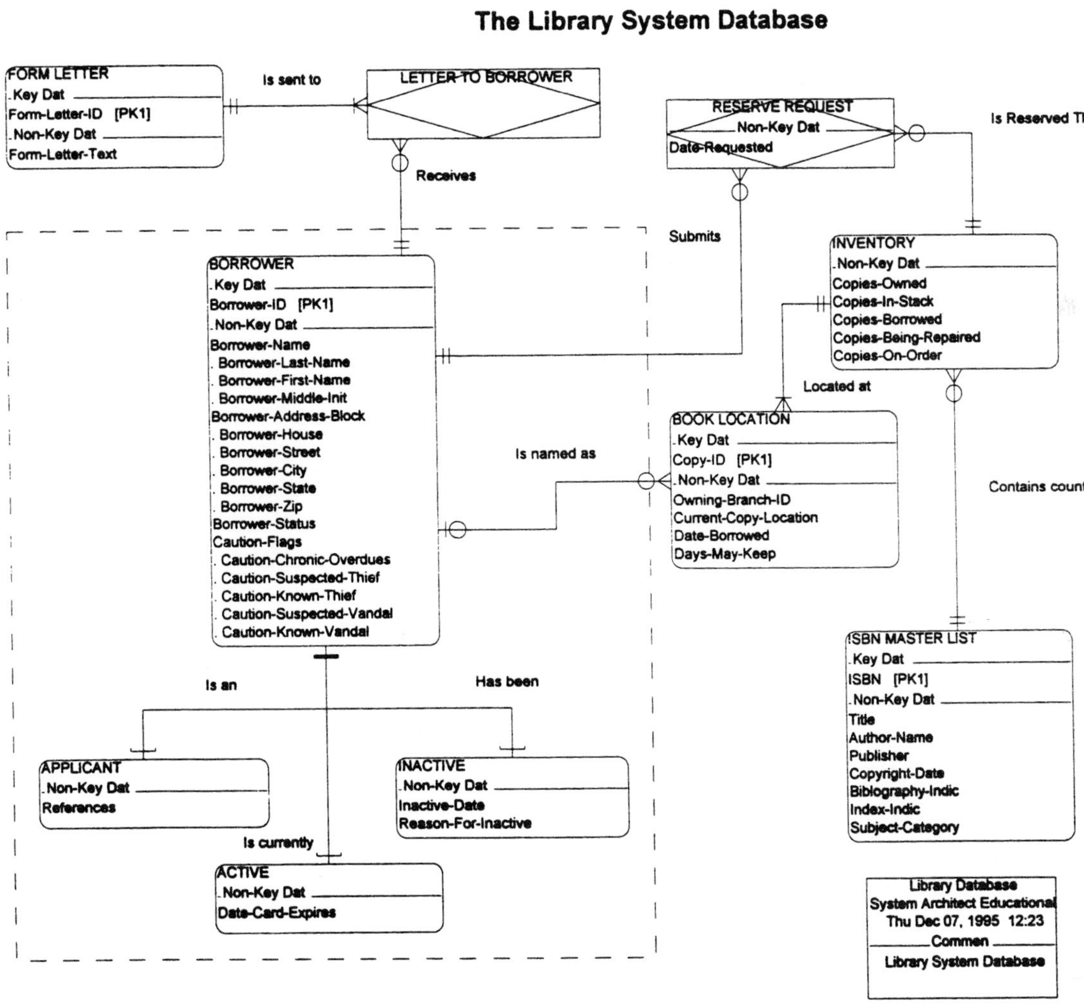

The Library System Database

Figure 8-1. Library System Data Model

8.1 Diagram Types

System Architect supports Entity Relation and IDEF1X diagrams[1]. A general description of the symbol category is provided in *Table 8-1*. The symbol may indicate something more specific. See the System Architect on-line help facility for a detailed description of each symbol.

System Architect supports several data-modeling strategies. The underlying concepts of most popular strategies are quite similar; however, there are many variations on the notation standards used. System Architect supports the Chen standard, in addition to the Information Engineering standard.

The term used to define relationships between entities is dependent on the methodology used. Information Engineering uses the term cardinality and others, such as SSADM, use the term relationship degrees. System Architect uses the generic term associative properties to denote the specific relationship notation carried on relationship lines. *Figure 8-2* shows the different data modeling notations supported by System Architect.

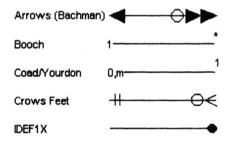

Figure 8-2. Relation Line Notation

---

[1] SSADM IV and OMT are also supported; see the System Architect on-line help facility for details.

Entity Relation Model	IDEF1X Model	Description
Entity	Independent Entity Dependent Entity	Entities represent database tables. Independent means it does not rely on other entities for its identification. Dependent entity always have at least one primary key that is a foreign key. Dependent Entity is the IDEF1X equivalent of the Weak Entity.
Associative Entity		An associative entity is a weak entity that exists for the sole purpose of resolving a many-to-many relationship. All of the primary keys of an associative entity are foreign keys, inherited from the entities for which the many-to-many relationship is resolved.
Weak Entity		A weak, or dependent entity depends on another entity for its existence. At least one of the primary keys will always be a foreign key.
	Complete Incomplete	A Category Discriminator is an attribute that categorizes generic parent instances. Complete means that all possible categories are displayed.
Access Path		The *access path*, sometimes referred to as an alternate index, represents an alternate way to read a given row from a table. The access path may, or may not, be a unique identifier.
Relation (one -to- zero, one, or more) (zero or one -to- one or more) (one -to- many) (Super -to- Sub)	Identifying Relation Z (one -to-zero or one) Nonidentifying Relation P (one -to- one or more) Nonspecific Relation (many -to- many)	Relation lines are used to specify the relationship between the data in two tables. Referential integrity constraints are specified in the Relationship definition.
Relation Diamond		The *Relation Diamond* is not in general use anymore. It allows you to depict *n-ary relationships*.
Data Element		The Data and Element symbols are essentially obsolete, but are included in System Architect for historical reasons. They are used to represent data structures and elements.

Table 8-1. Data Modeling Diagrams and Symbol Types

8.2 Drawing The ERD

The diagram we are about to draw in this section is a logical data model. If we were working on a real project, the model would be completely normalized. The steps in this section explain how to draw the model using System Architect: selecting the objects, placing them on the diagram, and defining them.

In general, the drawing techniques learned in chapters 3 and 4 on drawing a process model are the same as those required for a data model. However, since you might have skipped directly to this section, some steps are repeated. Although the Data model represents a very different aspect of the system than the Process model, the techniques used for drawing the two types of diagrams in System Architect (i.e., placing and connecting symbols) is essentially the same, with the exception of the Associative Properties dialog for the line symbols.

1. This section assumes you have completed *Chapter 2*, started System Architect, and opened the *Project1* encyclopedia. If you haven't, please do so at this time.

2. Pull down the **Diagram** menu and select the **New** command.

Figure 8-3. Preparing to Create a New Diagram

2. In the **Name** box type Library Database.

3. Select the diagram type **Entity Relation** from the diagram selection box below the **Name** box.

4. Click on the **OK** button. A blank drawing screen appears.

All menus except **Symbol** are now active; the **EntityRel** methodology menu is on the far right of the menu bar. It contains the symbol commands you need to draw entity relation diagrams, plus rules and normalization checking reports. These symbols are also accessible from the toolbox, displayed in the left margin of the window.

8.2.1 The System Architect Window

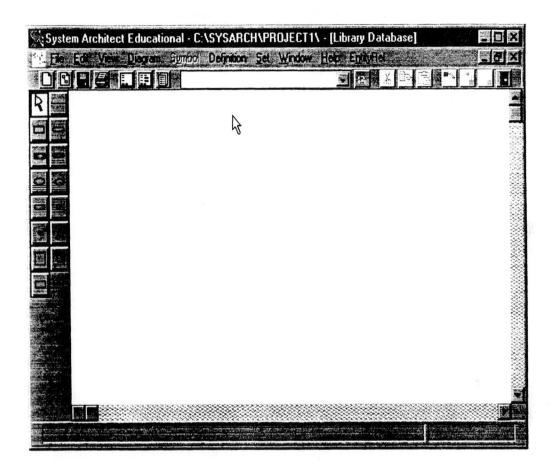

Figure 8-4. System Architect Window

System Architect provides a *Toolbar* and a *Toolbox*.

The Toolbar

Figure 8-5. The Toolbar

The System Architect toolbar appears below the menu bar at the top of the
System Architect window. The icons may be used to perform common drawing
functions. The name of each icon can be displayed by slowly moving the mouse
pointer over the icon.

The following table shows the icon, the menu equivalent, and a brief explanation of the action each performs.

Icon	Menu command	Action
	Diagram Menu New	Start a new diagram
	Diagram Menu Open	Open an existing diagram
	Diagram Menu Save	Save the diagram currently in focus
	File Menu Print	Print the diagram currently in focus
	Definition Menu Add	Add a new definition for any object supported by System Architect
	Definition Menu Modify	Modify any definition in the encyclopedia
	File Menu Reports	Load the report file in preparation for selecting a report to run.
FORM LETTER (Entity)	N/A	the Symbol Locate list box
	N/A	Rapid Locate
	Edit Menu Cut	Cut selected symbols from the diagram currently in focus.
	Edit Menu Copy	Copy selected symbols from the diagram currently in focus.
	Edit Menu Paste	Paste selected symbols or text from the Clipboard to the diagram in focus.
	Symbol Menu Child Open	Open and change focus to the child diagram of the currently selected symbol.
	Symbol Menu Parent	Open and change focus to the diagram of the parent symbol of the diagram currently in focus.
	Symbol Menu Top	Open and change focus to the diagram at the top of the leveled set of the diagram currently in focus.
	View Menu Toolbox	Toggle the Toolbox on and off. (This command affects diagrams of the type currently in focus.)

Icon	Menu command	Action
⚡	Edit Menu Route now	Route any selected lines of the Automatic orthogonal style.

Table 8-2. Icons on the Toolbar

Symbol Locate

The Symbol Locate list box can be used in two ways. If a symbol is selected, its name and type is displayed in the box. On the other hand, if you want to rapidly locate any symbol on a diagram, find its name in the list and select it. Then click on the binoculars. The focus of the diagram immediately shifts to the chosen symbol. The chosen view size of the diagram does not change.

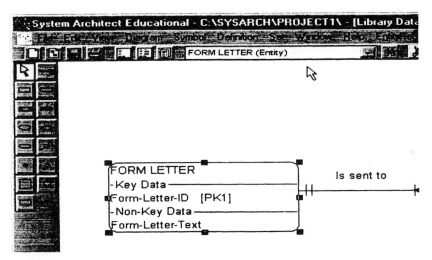

Figure 8-6. The name and symbol type in the Symbol Locate list box

The Toolbox

There is a unique Toolbox for every methodology menu. The tools in the Toolbox are specific to the methodology.

Figure 8-7. Toolbox for the Entity Relation Diagram

You can toggle the Toolbox on and off for individual diagrams by

- de-selecting **Toolbox** from the **View** menu,
- de-selecting **Toolbox** from the floating diagram menu[2], or
- clicking the Toolbox icon on the Toolbar.

The *Display Toolbox Preference* must be toggled on for the toolbox to be opened automatically with the diagram.

8.2.2 Window Size

Most people prefer drawing diagrams on a large screen. Click on the "maximize" button to obtain the largest possible work area

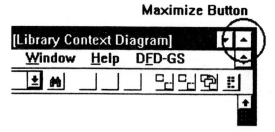

Figure 8-8. The Maximize Button

---

2 For information about floating menus, refer to *Section 5.6, Using Pop-up Menus.*

8.2.3 Reduction Percentage

When beginning a new diagram, System Architect will, by default, display the
actual size of the symbols on the screen. When you're drawing a large diagram,
the **Actual Size** option may not allow you to show a significant portion of the
diagram on your screen, and clarity may be lost with the **Used Area** option such
that you can't determine the names of your symbols.

You will often find drawing easier if you work on a moderately reduced scale.
From experience, we have found that a 75% reduction usually works well. This
is the System Architect default value for the reduced view. To change to 75%
reduction:

    1. Pull down the **View** menu.

    2. Click on **Reduced 75%**.

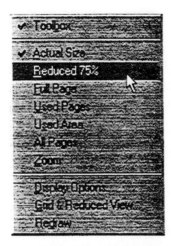

Figure 8-9. The **View** Menu

The percentage of reduction for the **Reduce _n_%** command (**Reduce 75%** in our
example) is specified using the **Grid & Reduced View** command.

8.2.3.1 Setting the Reduced View Percentage

The Grid & Reduced View command is used to change the percentage for
reducing the view.

The following procedure is used to specify the reduction percentage:

    1. Pull down the **View** menu.

    2. Click on the **Grid & Reduced View** command. The **Grid & Reduced
       View Settings** dialog appears.

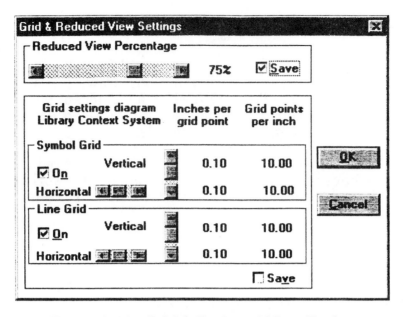

Figure 8-10. Grid & Reduced View Dialog

3. The horizontal scroll bar in the **Reduced View Percentage** box can be used to specify the percent reduction for the **Reduce *n*%** command in the **View** menu. We will leave this at the default value of 75%.

4. Click on **Save** in the **Reduced View Percentage** box to use the specified percent reduction as the default setting.

5. Click on **OK**.

8.2.4 Setting Your Session Preferences

Before starting the examples in this section of the manual, check the default settings in the **Preferences** dialog box. A complete explanation of each option is in *Appendix A*.

Click on the **Set** menu and select the **Preferences** command. Make sure *[Auto] Associate, [Auto] Define,* , and *[Create FK Report]* are toggled on. If the dialog box on your screen does not have the options toggled like those in *Figure 8-11* below, make whatever changes are necessary. Click on **Save** and **OK**.

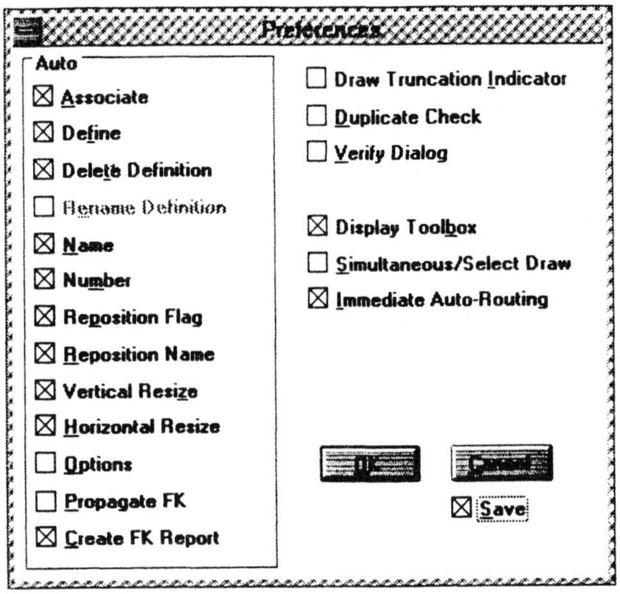

Figure 8-11. The **Preferences** Dialog Box for the exercises in this section of the Manual

8.2.5 Drawing an Entity

Hint Slowly drag your cursor over the Toolbox, without pressing the mouse button. The name of the symbol under the cursor is displayed in a small rectangle to the right of the icon of the tool. The Toolbar works the same way, displaying the action of the icon.

All rectangular symbols are drawn and placed in the same way.

1.  Pull down the **EntityRel** menu and select **Entity**, or select the Entity symbol from the Toolbox.

   The cursor changes to a "pencil and rectangle." The pencil indicates you are in "draw" mode, ready to place symbols in your diagram. The rectangle indicates a rectangular shaped symbol is to be drawn; an entity symbol in this case.[3]

_____

[3] In System Architect, the term "rectangular symbol" is used to indicate symbols that are not linear.

Figure 8-12. Cursor in Draw Mode

2. Move the cursor to the approximate place on the drawing area where you would like the symbol to appear and click on the left mouse button. An entity symbol appears above and to the left of the cursor. Do not release the mouse button.

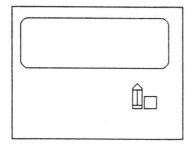

Figure 8-13. The entity symbol and the cursor in its drawing shape

Continue to hold down the left button and move the mouse, "dragging" the entity symbol across the screen. Notice that the symbol moves with the mouse.

Hint System Architect orients the symbol on an invisible grid as you move it.

3. Drag the entity symbol about an inch below the top of the visible portion of the diagram, and an inch to the right of the left-hand margin, and release the mouse button, anchoring it.

   If you want to move the symbol after it's anchored, see *Chapter 5, Editing Symbols and Lines.*

4. The **Add Symbol (Entity)** dialog box is displayed. Type FORM LETTER in the **Name** text box.

Add Symbol (Entity)	
Name FORM LETTER	
Graphic Comment	

Figure 8-14. Enter the name in the **Add Symbol [Entity]** Dialog Box

5. Click on **OK**.

6. The next dialog displayed is the **Add Definition [Entity]** dialog because the *Auto Define* preference was specified..

8.2.5.1 Adding Data Entity Attributes

The cursor is automatically in the Attributes text box. Enter the names of the attributes (or data) of the entity.

1. Type the name of the first attribute, Form-Letter-ID, preceding it with an @, and hit the Enter key.

   The @ indicates the attribute is the prime key, or part of the prime key. A space between the @ and the name is optional.

2. Type the name of the next attribute, Form-Letter-Text.

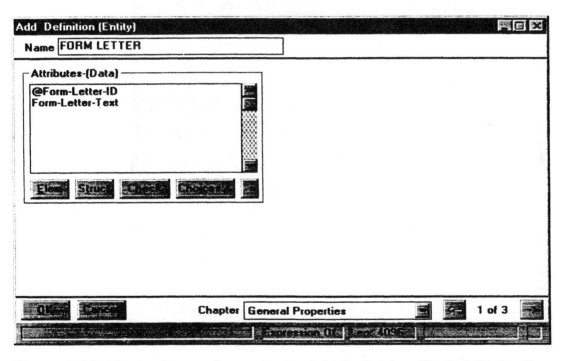

Figure 8-15. Enter the attributes in the **Add Definition [Entity]** Dialog Box

3. Proceed to the next section.

8.2.5.2 Defining an Entity's Data Elements

Most of the following data elements may already be defined if you completed the chapters on process modeling previous to this chapter. For those elements already defined, click **OK** and continue to the next definition.

1. Select the words *Form-Letter-ID* in the data text box by double-clicking, and click on the **Elem** button at the bottom of the box.

2. The **Add Definition (Data Element)** dialog is displayed. Enter the
    description in the Description text box as shown below in *Figure 8-
    16*, and click on **OK**.

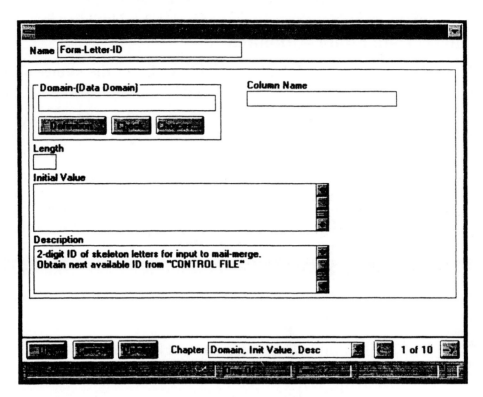

Figure 8-16. The **Add Definition (Data Element)** Dialog

3. Repeat steps 1 and 2 for the second data element, *Form-Letter-Text*
    with a description, `Skeleton letters in format suitable`
    `for mail merge.`

4. Click on **OK** in the *FORM LETTERS* entity dialog.

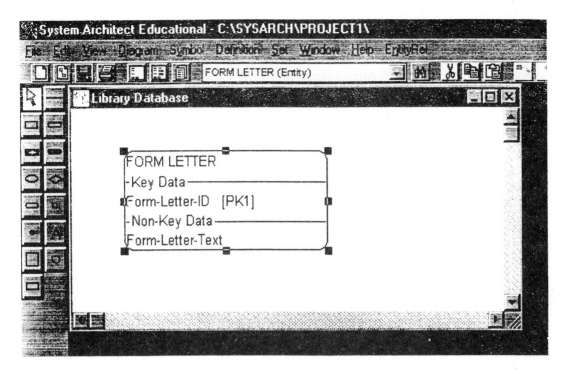

Figure 8-17. The Library Database ERD so far.

8.3 Saving a Diagram

Save your work frequently, using the **Save** command from the **Diagram** menu,
or the **Save Diagram** button on the toolbar. Changes to a diagram are not
recorded in the encyclopedia until the diagram is saved. Therefore, if you were
to lose power to your PC, all the work you have done since opening the diagram
(or from your last save) will be lost.

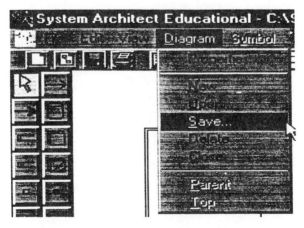

Figure 8-18. The **Diagram** Menu

8.4 Exiting System Architect

There are three ways to exit System Architect:

- Pull down the **File** menu, and click on the **Exit** command.

Figure 8-19. The **File** Menu

- Double-click on the *Control-menu box*.

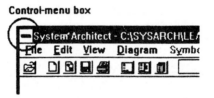

Figure 8-20. The Control-Menu Box

- Single-click on the *Control-menu box*, then click on the **Close** command in the Control menu.

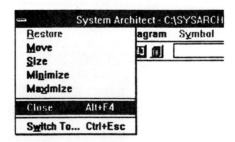

Figure 8-21. The Control Menu

8.5 Questions in Review

1. Define a weak entity.

2. Define an access path.

3. List two ways the Symbol Locate list box can be used.

4. True or False: There is a unique toolbox for every methodology menu.

5. List three ways to toggle the Toolbox on or off.

6. What is System Architect's default value for reduced view?

7. List two techniques to change the cursor to a "pencil and rectangle" in order to draw an entity symbol.

8. When defining an entity's attributes, what does the @ sign indicate?

9. True or False: System Architect automatically saves changes to a diagram as soon as they occur.

10. List three ways to exit System Architect.

Answers to the above questions can be found in Appendix B.

9. Completing The ERD

In this section we are going to finish the ERD for the Library data base started in *Chapter 8.* The diagram is shown in *Figure 9-1.*

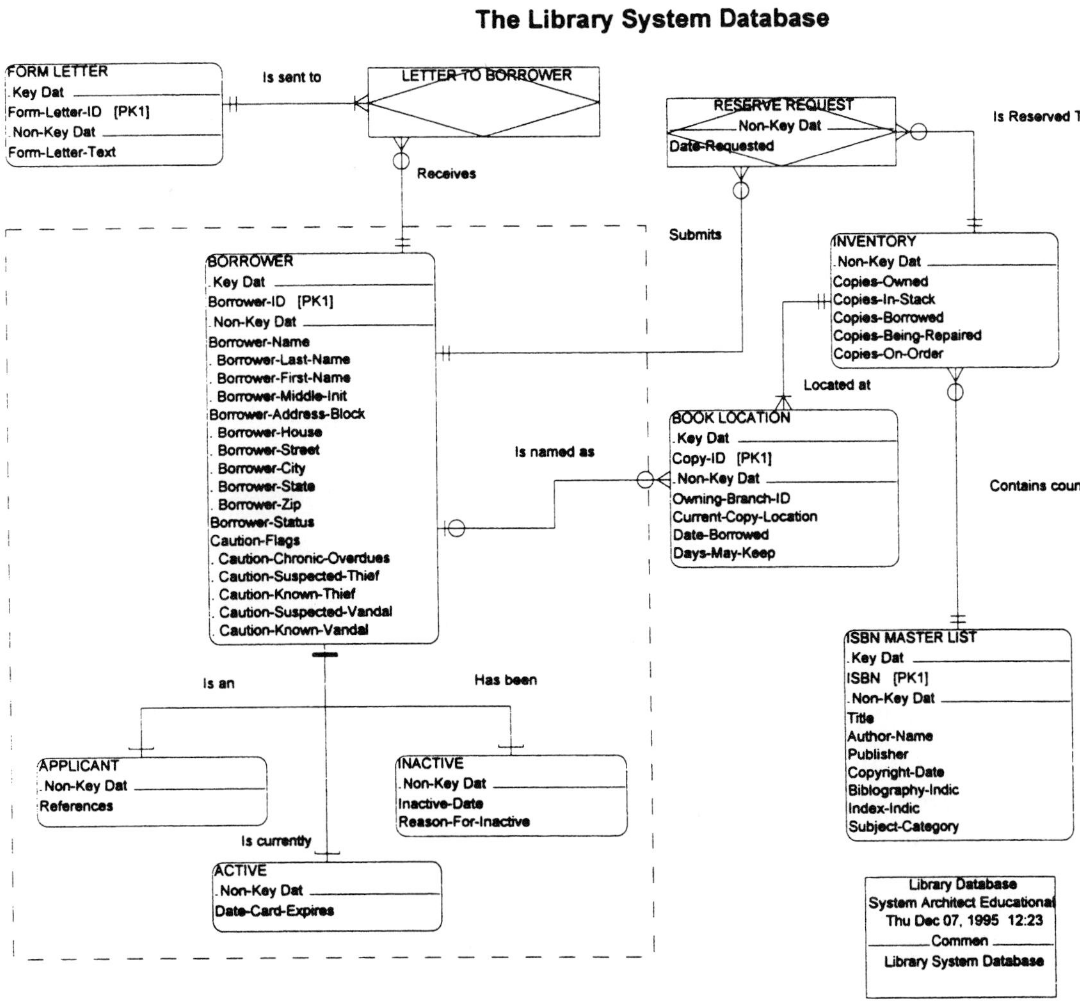

The Library System Database

Figure 9-1. Library System Data Model

9.1 Opening a Diagram

This section assumes you have started System Architect and opened the *Project1* encyclopedia. If you haven't, please do so at this time.

1. Pull down the **Diagram** menu and click **Open**. The *Select For Opening* dialog will be displayed.

2. Select *Entity Relation* in the **Type** list box then click **Search**.

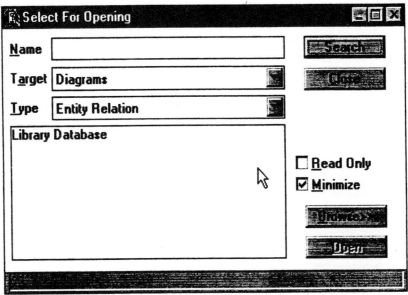

Figure 9-2. The Open Diagram Dialog

3. System Architect will search for all diagrams of the Entity Relation type and list them in the text box. Select the *Library Database* diagram and click **Open**.

   The Library Database diagram is displayed.

9.2 Adding The Remaining Entities

ERD's must contain entity[1] symbols, connected by relation lines. In addition, entities may be designated as super or sub. Sub-entities represent categorizations of the super-entity type. For example, in the Library System, there are 3 kinds of borrowers:

---

[1] Any entity can be categorized as entity, associative entity, or weak entity. The symbols are slightly different looking, but each represents an object in the system.

- those who regularly borrow books from the library -- the *active* borrowers;

- those who haven't borrowed any books in a year -- the *inactive* borrowers; and

- those who would like to be able to borrow books, but haven't been approved by the Library Committee -- the *applicant* borrowers.[2]

Hint To see more of the drawing space of the diagram at once, change the area viewed. From the **View** Menu, select *Reduce 75%*, or *Full Page*.

To add the BORROWER entity, take the following steps:

1. Hold the left mouse button down, creating another entity symbol. Drag it below FORM LETTER, and slightly to the right. Release the left mouse button.

2. Enter the name of the new entity, BORROWER.

3. Enter the attributes of the entity, as pictured in *Figure 9-3*.

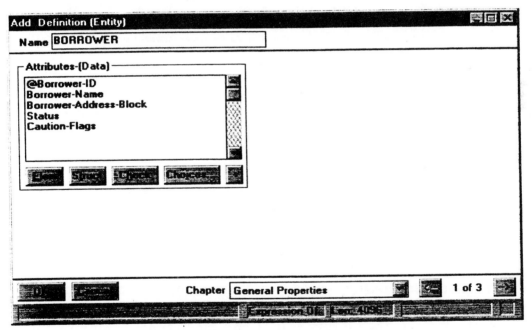

Figure 9-3. The BORROWERS entity

4. Define each of the attributes by repeating the procedure discussed in *Section 8.2.5.2*. Reference *Tables 9-1 through 9-3* to determine the type of each attribute, whether data element or structure, and the

---

2 Expressions such as "haven't borrowed in a year," and "haven't been approved by the committee" are considered business rules. ERD's, in addition to picturing the relationship between things in the system, explicate business rules.

description of each element. If the attribute is a data structure refer to the next step.

5. The second attribute in the BORROWER entity is Borrower-Name. It is a data structure, not a data element. Select it, and click on the *Struct* button.

   Enter the names of its attributes as pictured below.

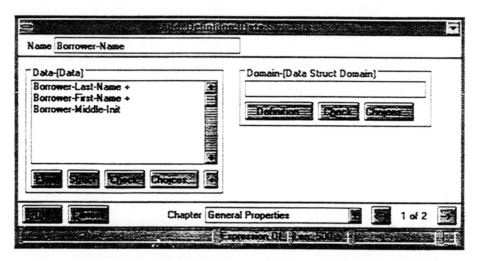

Figure 9-4. The Borrower-Name data structure

6. Define each of the data elements by selecting each one and clicking the **Elem** button. Enter the description of the data element found in *Table 9-3*.

Hint The diagram picture is not saved automatically. From time to time, click on the Diagram Save icon on the toolbar, or select **Save** from the **Diagram** Menu. When the *Save Diagram <diagram name>* query is displayed, click on **Yes**.

 An *Associative Entity* is used to resolve many-to-many relationships. For example, in the Public Library we are modeling, borrowers are sent letters by the Library staff from time to time, reminding them of overdue books, asking for money for fund-raising, and so on. That is, any given letter is sent to many borrowers, and one borrower receives many letters, alternatively expressed as

     many BORROWERS Receive many LETTERS.

The Library System has 5 entities:
- BOOK LOCATION
- BORROWER
- FORM LETTER
- INVENTORY
- ISBN MASTER LIST

The BORROWER entity has 3 sub-entities:
- APPLICANT
- ACTIVE
- INACTIVE

Sub-entities are drawn using the entity symbol. You will identify them as sub-entities when you draw the relation lines in a later section.

The Library System has 2 associative entities:
- LETTER TO BORROWER
- RESERVE REQUEST

LETTER TO BORROWER resolves a many-to-many relationship between BORROWER and FORM LETTER. RESERVE REQUEST resolves a many-to-many relationship between BORROWER and INVENTORY.

In order to draw the remaining entities, and add the necessary definitions, you need the following information listed in *Tables 9-1, 9-2, and 9-3*. A picture of the completed diagram is shown in *Figure 9-1* -- use it for the placement of the entities. After all the entities have been drawn, we will add the relation lines.

1. Complete the drawing of the entities now.

Entity	Contains	
ACTIVE	data element	Date-Card-Expires
APPLICANT	data structure	References
BOOK LOCATION	data element	Copy-ID
	data element	Owning-Branch-ID
	data element	Current-Copy-Location
	data element	Date-Borrowed
	data element	Days-May-Keep
BORROWER	data element	Borrower-ID
	data structure	Borrower-Name
	data structure	Borrower-Address-Block
	data element	Status
	data structure	Caution-Flags
FORM LETTER	data element	Form-Letter-ID
	data element	Form-Letter-Text
INACTIVE	data element	Inactive-Date

Entity	Contains	
INVENTORY	data element	Copies-Owned
	data element	Copies-In-Stacks
	data element	Copies-Borrowed
	data element	Copies-Being-Repaired
	data element	Copies-On-Order
ISBN MASTER LIST	data element	ISBN
	data element	Title
	data element	Author-Name
	data element	Copyright-Date
	data element	Publisher
	data element	Bibliography-Indic
	data element	Index-Indic
	data element	Subject-Category
LETTER TO BORROWER	data element	Date-Letter-Sent
RESERVE REQUEST	data element	Date-Requested

Table 9-1. Entities and Attributes in the Library Database Diagram

Data Structure Name	Component Data
Borrower-Address-Block	Borrower-House
	Borrower-Street
	Borrower-City
	Borrower-State
	Borrower-ZIP
Borrower-Name	Borrower-Last-Name
	Borrower-First-Name
	Borrower-Middle-Init
Caution-Flags	Caution-Chronic-Overdues
	Caution-Suspected-Thief
	Caution-Known-Thief
	Caution-Suspected-Vandal
	Caution-Known-Vandal
New-Borrower-Data	Borrower-ID
	Borrower-Name
	Borrower-Address-Block
	References
Reference-Address-Block	Reference-House
	Reference-Street
	Reference-City
	Reference-State
	Reference-ZIP
References	Reference-Name
	Reference-Address-Block
	Reference-Description
Reserve-Book-Data	ISBN
	Date-Requested

Table 9-2. Data Structures used in the Library Database entities

Data Element	Description
Author-Name	Author of book
Bibliography-Indic	Does this book have a bibliography?
Borrower-City	self-explanatory
Borrower-First-Name	self-explanatory
Borrower-House	Borrower house number.
Borrower-ID	If possible, user borrower's SSN else use the next available ID.
Borrower-Last-Name	self-explanatory
Borrower-Middle-Init	self-explanatory
Borrower-State	Use standard postal 2-letter codes.
Borrower-Street	self-explanatory
Borrower-ZIP	5 or 9 character zip.
Caution-Chronic-Overdues	5 or more overdues in prior 12 months
Caution-Known-Thief	self-explanatory
Caution-Known-Vandal	self-explanatory
Caution-Suspected-Thief	self-explanatory
Caution-Suspected-Vandal	self-explanatory
Copies-Being-Repaired	Number of copies of this book currently at bindery for repair.
Copies-Borrowed	Number of copies of this book in hands of borrowers.
Copies-In-Stacks	Number of copies of this book available for lending.
Copies-On-Order	Number of copies of this book back-ordered from publisher.
Copies-Owned	Number of copies of this book owned by the library system as of 10/04/95.
Copy-ID	Unique sequential number assigned to each new copy of any given book when added to the library inventory. Derive the number to assign by scanning "INVENTORY FILE" for numbers already used. Do not reuse numbers. Always assign the next number one greater than the biggest one so far.
Copyright-Date	Copyright data of the book in question.
Current-Copy-Location	Location of the book in question. Valid choices are: 1. In the stacks of Main or one of the 5 branches 2. Borrowed by "Borrower-ID" 3. At the BINDERY for repair
Date-Borrowed	self-explanatory
Date-Card-Expires	self-explanatory
Date-Letter-Sent	self-explanatory
Date-Requested	Date user asked a book to be reserved for them.

Data Element	Description
Days-May-Keep	Usually 14 days, but may differ for certain reference books. Date is stamped inside the cover.
Inactive-Date	Date borrower became inactive.
Index-Indic	Does this book have an index?
ISBN	International standard book number.
Owning-Branch-ID	Branch book in question was assigned to. Borrower may return any book to any branch, but every attempt should be made to return a book back to its owning branch.
Publisher	Publisher of the book in question.
Reference-City	self-explanatory
Reference-Description	Type of reference (employer, school, teacher, doctor, etc.)
Reference-House	self-explanatory
Reference-Name	self-explanatory
Reference-State	Use standard postal 2-letter codes.
Reference-Street	self-explanatory
Reference-ZIP	5 or 9 character zip.
Status	None
Subject-Category	Subject (s) of the book in question
Title	Title of the book in question

Table 9-3. Descriptions of data elements

9.3 Drawing Lines Connecting Symbols

Lines connecting symbols have different meanings, depending on the modeling method chosen. In entity relation diagrams, for example, lines are called *relation lines* and represent the relationship between entities. The relationship is usually expressed in a verb phrase, read from the source entity to the target entity: BORROWER Submits RESERVE REQUEST.

In System Architect the techniques for drawing all lines, regardless of the methodology you are using and what is represented, are the same..

9.3.1 Available Line Types

System Architect supports four different line types. The differences are summarized in the following table:

Cursor shape when selected	Line type	Characteristics
	Straight, any orientation	Does not require bend points, but lines can be bent at any angle.[3]
	Straight orthogonal	To switch direction must have 1 or more bend points.[4]
	Automatic orthogonal	Exactly like straight orthogonal, but System Architect determines the bend points for you.
	Elliptical arc	Curved line between rectangular symbols.

Table 9-4. Supported Line Styles

Of the four line styles available in System Architect, only *Straight orthogonal* and *Automatic orthogonal* are appropriate for data models.

We will use *Automatic (orthogonal)* lines for this example. You can specify this as the default line style. To set your line style default:

1. Pull down the **Set** menu.

2. Choose the **Line** command.

3. Set the *Automatic (orthogonal)* option to **ON**.

4. Ensure the **Round Corners** option is <u>not</u> checked.

5. Set the **Save** option to **ON**; the new setting will be saved as the default setting.

6. Click on **OK**.

---

[3] If you're familiar with the game of chess, this line type moves like the Queen, it that it can go any direction it wants (providing a bendpoint is placed where the direction is changed).

[4] This line type moves like the rook, it can go straight across, but requires a bendpoint to change direction.

9.3.2 Drawing Relation Lines

1. ![icon] Pull down the **EntityRel** menu and select the **Relation** command, or select the relation line from the Toolbox.

   ![pencil icon] The cursor now has changed to the "draw" mode indicator "pencil" shape. Notice the lightning bolt next to the pencil, the visual indicator of the Automatic Orthogonal style.

2. Place the pencil point *inside* the FORM LETTER entity symbol, the source of the relationship. It is not necessary to try to start the line precisely on the side of the symbol; place it well inside the symbol and System Architect will make sure it is connected.

   If the handle is inside the symbol, it appears as a cross. If it is outside the symbol, it appears as a box.

☞ *Relation lines on Entity Relation diagrams should always be started at the source entity and ended at the target entity because the source/target designation cannot be changed. If the line is inadvertently started at the target entity, it is better to delete it and start again.*

3. Click the left mouse button once to start the line.

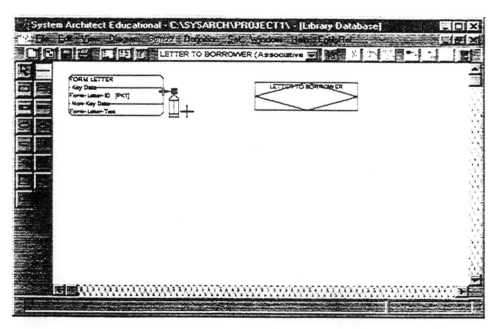

Figure 9-5. Start to Draw the Line from *Inside* the Starting Symbol

4. Do not drag the mouse across the diagram. Instead, place it inside the LETTER TO BORROWER entity, the target symbol, and click the left mouse button once.

The line is attached to the symbol at the chosen point.

Hint If you want to stop drawing a line before you have attached it at both ends to a symbol, press the Escape key. The line disappears and the cursor changes to a pointer shape. To begin another line, you will have to select the **Relation** command again.

9.3.2.1 Is The Line Anchored In Place?

Relation lines on data models are, traditionally, anchored at both ends: the source entity and the target entity (or access path). To check if the line is anchored, select it, and check the first and last handles against the pictures below. If one of the ends is not anchored, simply grab the unanchored end and drag it inside the appropriate entity.

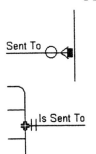

Filled-in square: this end is not anchored.

Cross-shaped: this end is anchored.

9.3.3 Adding The Relationship Name, Definition, and Properties

Now the name, definition, and properties of the relationship are added.

1. The **Add Symbol (Relation)** dialog box is displayed. Type the name `Is sent to` in the **Name** box. Click on **OK**.

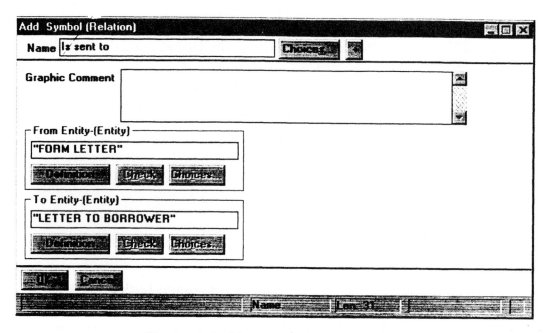

Figure 9-6. Naming a Relation Line

2. Click on **OK**.

3. The next dialog displayed is the definition dialog, into which you can enter the description appropriate for that relation. Click on **OK** without entering anything.

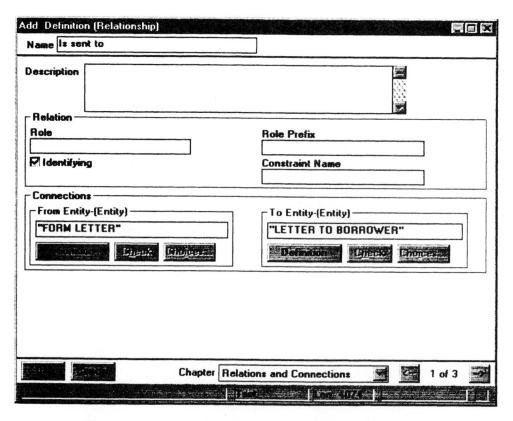

Figure 9-7. The **Add Definition [Relation]** Dialog

4. The **Associative Properties** dialog box is displayed next because the *Auto Associate* preference is specified.

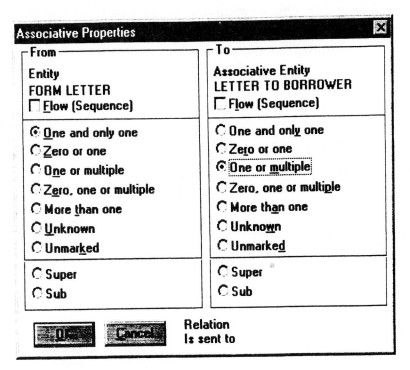

Figure 9-8. Cardinality for a Relation Line

5. The *cardinality* of the source (or *from*) entity, FORM LETTER is *One and only one*. Click on that radio button in the dialog.

6. The *cardinality* of the target entity, LETTERS TO BORROWERS, is *One or multiple*. Click on that radio button in the dialog.

7. Click on **OK**.

A short discussion of cardinality on relation lines

The choices *One and only one, One or multiple,* and *More than one* indicate that the entity is mandatory. *Zero or one, Zero, one or multiple,* and *Unknown* indicate the entity is optional. The optional/mandatory property is indicated on the relation line through the use of a circle (or O) or a small straight line, respectively.

If the source entity is *One and only one,* or *One or multiple,* it is commonly referred to as the parent. The child entity is usually *One or multiple,* or *Zero, one or multiple.*

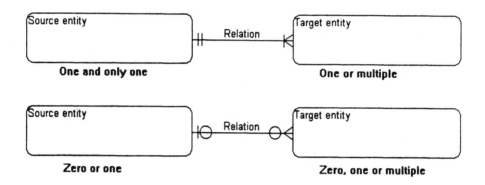

Figure 9-9. Cardinality and optional/mandatory indications

9.3.4 Subtypes and Supertypes

To indicate a super/sub-entity relationship:

1. Use BORROWER as the source symbol and draw a relation line to APPLICANT.

2. Complete the associative dialog as pictured in *Figure 9-10* below.

   System Architect draws a dotted line rectangle around the super and sub-entities, pictorially setting them apart from the rest of the diagram, and indicating their special relationship.

3. Add a super/sub relationship from BORROWER to ACTIVE and INACTIVE.

   The dotted line rectangle increases in size as necessary to enclose all the entities in this relationship.

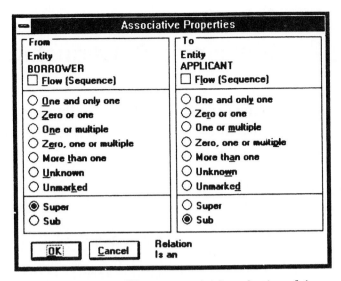

Figure 9-10. The super/sub relationship

In order to tidy up the super/sub relationship lines so they look like the completed diagram in *Figure 9-1*, follow these steps.

1. Select all three of the lines between BORROWER and the three sub-entities, by holding the Shift key down while you click on the lines.

2. From the **Set** Menu, select the **Line** command. Click on *Straight orthogonal*.

3. Select each line in turn. Move the source point of the line in the BORROWER entity to the bottom border of BORROWER, if necessary. Make sure the handle remains attached to BORROWER, it must be cross-shaped, not a solid box.

4. Grab any handle on the lines to move them to overlap at the source point

5. If necessary, add additional bend points, selecting **Insert Line Segment** from the **Line** pop up Menu.

System Architect places line names adjacent to one of the middle bend points of a multi-segment line; this place is not always the best place for a name. Instructions for moving line names are in *Chapter 5 Editing Symbols and Lines*.

9.3.5 Drawing The Remaining Relationship Lines

1. Complete the drawing of the Entity Relation diagram, adding the remaining relationship lines, as in the complete diagram in *Figure 9-1*. Use *Table 9-5* for a listing of the relationship lines.

Source Entity	Relationship	Target Entity
BOOK LOCATION	Located At	INVENTORY
BORROWER	Is currently	ACTIVE
	Is an	APPLICANT
	Is Named As	BOOK LOCATION
	Has been	INACTIVE
	Receives	LETTERS TO BORROWERS
	Submits	RESERVE REQUEST
FORM LETTER	Is Sent To	LETTERS TO BORROWERS
INVENTORY	Contains Counts Of	ISBN MASTER LIST
	Is Reserved Through	RESERVE REQUEST

Table 9-5. Library Database relationship lines

9.4 Diagram Standards

Most organizations have standards and guidelines for drawing diagrams. Two commonly used standards include:

- The placement of a title descriptive of the diagram at the top of each diagram page. The **Text** command can be used to create titles or other text annotations.

- The inclusion of each diagram name and the date on which it was created or last revised. The **Doc Block** command can be used to place a rectangular symbol containing the diagram name and creation/last modification date. System Architect automatically changes the date and time every time a diagram is modified. The date and time, and other important information can be included as a comment in the Doc Block.

9.4.1 Placing Free-Form Text

The **Text** command is used to add single lines, or multiple-line-blocks, of text to a diagram. Once the text is created, it can be placed on the diagram, moved, and deleted in the same manner as a rectangular symbol. Additionally, text can be enhanced by changing its font type, size, and style.

To place a title on a diagram:

1. 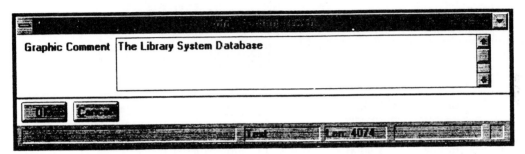 Pull down the methodology menu (in this case, **Entity-Rel**) and select the **Text** command, or click the Text symbol in the toolbox. The **Add Symbol (Text)** dialog will open.

2. Enter your text, The Library System Database.

Graphic Comment | The Library System Database

Figure 9-11. Enter the diagram title.

3. Click on **OK** once the text has been entered. The **Add Symbol (Text)** dialog will close and the drawing cursor will change to a drawing pencil with an *A* next to it. This indicates System Architect is ready to place your text block.

4. Press and hold down the left mouse button. A dotted rectangle appears in the shape of your entered text. This method is the same used to place any other rectangular symbol.

Figure 9-12. Positioning Free-Form Text

5. While continuing to hold down the mouse button, drag the dotted rectangle into place.

6. Release the mouse button. Your text appears.

9.4.2 Changing The Font Style

To change the font "style" of text which has already been placed:

1. Confirm that you are in the select mode. If you are in the draw mode, or if you are unsure of what mode you are in, click your left mouse button on the *Cursor* button in the toolbox.

2. Select the text by clicking the left mouse button on top of it. The text block will change to reverse video when selected.

3. Pull down the **Set** menu and select the **Font** command. The **Font Style** dialog will open.

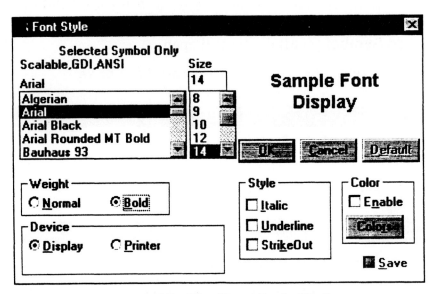

Figure 9-13. The **Font Style** Dialog

4. Select your font name and point size from the scrolling lists and also make your weight and style choices. The effect of each choice is reflected in the sample text window. For this example use the following settings:

   - Font   Arial
   - Point Size   14
   - Weight   Bold

5. Click on **OK**. The text block will change to reflect your font choices.

6. Click anywhere on the diagram in white space to deselect the title.

9.5 Adding a Doc Block

Use the **Doc Block** command to add a documentation block to your diagram. This symbol will contain the encyclopedia name of your diagram and the current date and time. It should be placed in a standard place on all diagrams - for example, in the lower right hand corner.

Place the doc block as you would any other rectangular symbol. Also, it can be resized, moved, and deleted just like any other rectangular symbol.
To place a doc block on your diagram, do the following:

1. 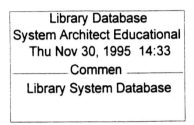 Pull down the methodology menu (**Entity-Rel**) and choose the **Doc Block** command, or click the *Doc Block* symbol in the toolbox. The drawing cursor changes to the familiar pen-and-rectangle shape indicating drawing mode.

2. Place the doc block as you would any other rectangular symbol.

> Library Database
> System Architect Educational
> Thu Nov 30, 1995 14:33
> ———— Commen ————
> Library System Database

Figure 9-14. The Doc Block

To add a comment to the Doc block:

1. Select the Doc Block by clicking the left mouse button on it.

2. Pull down the **Symbol** menu.

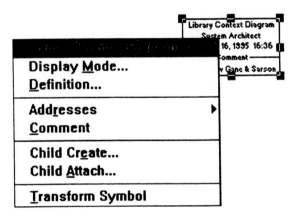

Figure 9-15. The floating menu

4. Select the **Name, Number, Properties** command.

5. Enter any appropriate comments, as pictured below then click **OK**.

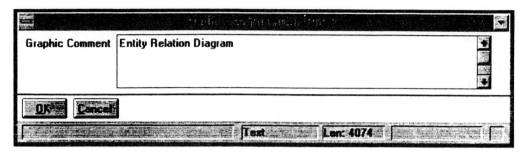

Figure 9-16. The **Modify Symbol (Doc Block)** dialog

9.6 Using Display Mode

The **Display Mode** command allows the user to display definition information directly on the diagram. Several definition properties can be specified for each rectangular symbol. The values can be selectively displayed and printed inside the symbol boundaries.

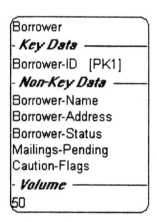

Figure 9-17.   Displaying Definition Information on ER Diagram

To display or hide property information about each entity, do the following:

1. Select an entity symbol.

2. Pull down the **Symbol** menu.

3. Choose the **Display Mode** command. The **Display Mode** dialog will be opened; this dialog consists of seven options for the display of entities.

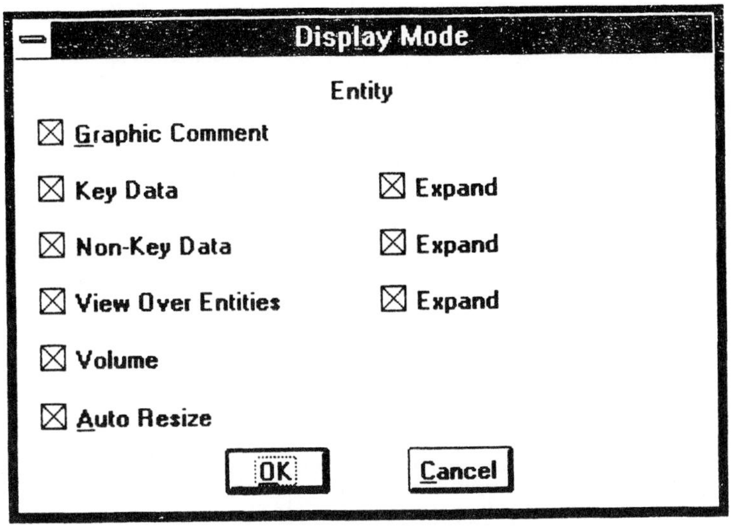

Figure 9-18. The **Display Mode** Dialog

The **Graphic Comment**, **Key Data**, **Non-Key Data**, **View Over Entities**, and **Volume** check boxes are used to specify whether or not to display the respective properties on the diagram. The **Expand** check boxes are used to specify whether or not to display the names of the data elements used by the data structures that define the entity. If the **Auto Resize**[5] check box is checked, System Architect will automatically resize the entity symbol on the ER diagram; the symbol size will be increased when you specify additional properties to be displayed, and reduced when you specify for properties not to be displayed.

4. Turn the options on or off by clicking on the check boxes.

5. Click on **OK** to save your changes and return to your ER diagram.

---

[5] The Auto Resize options (**Vertical Resize** and **Horizontal Resize**) must be enabled in the Preferences dialog (**Set** menu, **Preferences** command).

```
Borrower
-Key Data ─────────────
Borrower-ID  [PK1]
-Non-Key Data ─────────
Borrower-Name
. Borrower-Last-Name
. Borrower-First-Name
. Borrower-Middle-Init
Borrower-Address
. Borrower-Street
. Borrower-City
. Borrower-State
. Borrower-ZIP
Borrower-Status
Mailings-Pending
. Form-Letter-ID
Caution-Flags
. Caution-Chronic-Overdues
. Caution-Suspected-Thief
. Caution-Known-Thief
. Caution-Suspected-Vandal
. Caution-Known-Vandal
-Volume ────────────
50
```

Figure 9-17 Entity Showing Definition

9.7 Printing The Diagram

The **Print** command allows the user to print the current diagram.

To print the ERD currently displayed in the active window:

1. Pull down the **File** menu and select the **Page Settings** command.

2. Select the option to draw a simple border around the diagram and click on the *Best Fit* option. Click **OK**.

3. Pull down the **File** menu and select the **Print** command.

4. The diagram will be printed to the default printer selected.

☞   *Please note that the printer options that are changed in System Architect using the **Page Setup** dialog in the **File** menu are not permanent changes to the printer setup. Your printer setup is controlled by Windows.*

9.8 Saving a Diagram

Save your work frequently, using the **Save** command from the **Diagram** menu, or the **Save Diagram** button on the toolbar. Changes to a diagram are not recorded in the encyclopedia until the diagram is saved. Therefore, if you were to lose power to your PC, all the work you have done since opening the diagram (or from your last save) will be lost.

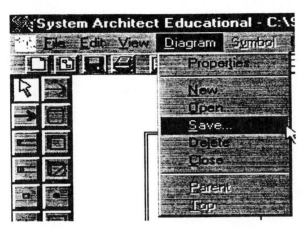

Figure 9-20. The **Diagram** Menu

9.9 Questions in Review

1. What is a sub-entity?

2. Define an associative entity.

3. List the available line types and their characteristics offered with System Architect.

4. Which two line types are appropriate to use for data models?

5. List the two methods to enter "drawing mode" in order to draw relation lines.

6. Why must relation lines always be started at the source entity and end at the target entity?

7. What key would you press to stop drawing a line before it is attached and return to "select mode."

8. The cardinality of a relation line is specified using which dialog box?

9. When System Architect draws a dotted line which encompasses two more entities, what does that signify?

10. What does the **Display Mode** command allow you to do?

Answers to the above questions can be found in Appendix B.

10. Running Data Modeling Reports

The System Architect Reporting System allows the user to specify queries and reports using information stored in the project dictionary. System Architect provides over one hundred pre-written reports that cover a wide range of project reporting requirements.

10.1 Running a report

The purpose of this section is to demonstrate how the pre-written reports are run. These reports are included on the System Architect program diskette that you received with the product at the time of purchase. If the recommended installation was followed, the reports will be found in the REPORTS.RPT file contained in the same directory as the System Architect executable module, usually C:\SYSARCH.

This section assumes you have started System Architect and opened the *Project1* encyclopedia. If you haven't, please do so at this time.

The following procedure is used to run a report to produce a listing of diagrams within the *Project1* encyclopedia.

1. Pull down the **File** menu, and select the **Reports** command. System Architect will take a minute to load the default report files; a selection box will then appear containing a list of available reports contained in the selected reports file.

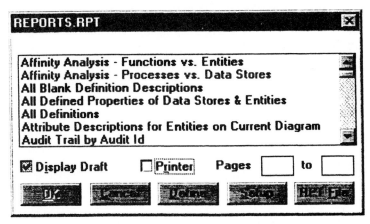

Figure 10-1. Selecting a Report form the REPORTS.RPT File

For this manual we are using the REPORTS.RPT file; the file may be changed by clicking on the **RPT File** button, located on the lower right hand corner of the **Reports** dialog, and selecting a new file.

2. Select the report named *Diagram Listing by Name* by scrolling the dialog box to its location and clicking the left mouse button on it.

3. Since we will not be printing the report now, click the left mouse button once in the **Printer** check box; it will become empty.   The printer box is a three-phase control box; it will either be empty, contain an X or check-mark, or be grayed. The report will not be sent to the printer if the box is empty. The report will always be printed if the box contains an X or check-mark, and the default print settings will be used if the box is grayed.

4. Select the **Display Draft** check box to place an X or check-mark in it. The output will be displayed in draft format on your screen.

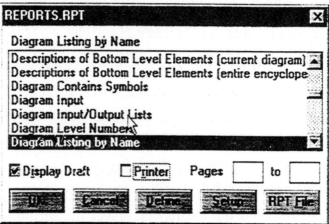

Figure 10-2. The **REPORTS.RPT** Dialog Window

5. Click on **OK** to run the report

The resulting "draft" report may look something like the following:

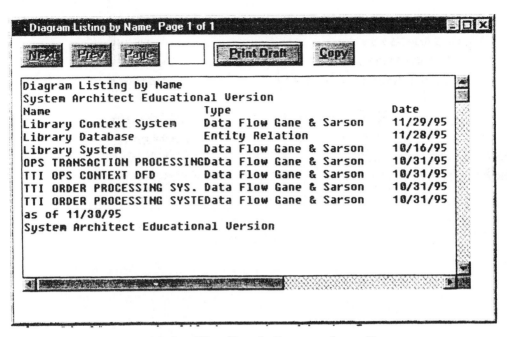

Figure 10-3. The Draft Output for a Report

6. Close the report window.

Formatting, such as bold text, only appears when the output is routed directly to the printer. It will not be shown on this display. A draft report can be composed much quicker than a fully-formatted printout. Font commands, such as *bold* or *italic* are ignored when creating a draft report. Format commands, such as *width*, and graphics commands, such as *underline* or *draw borders*, are also ignored.

10.2 Locating the Correct Pre-written Report

Over one-hundred reports are available to choose from in the selection box; therefore, it may be difficult to locate the report that will meet specific requirements.

1. The reports are listed in the **Reports** dialog in alphabetical order by report name. To quickly scroll to a report that is not in the initial window, select any report and press the keyboard key corresponding to the first letter of the report title to be retrieved. The first report title starting with that letter will be scrolled to and selected. Repeat pressing the same letter key until the desired report is visible, or use the slide bar located on the right side of the title window.

10.3 System Architect Rule-Checking Reports

System Architect provides a comprehensive set of rule-checking reports for examining the quality of both process and data models. These rule-checking programs look at the diagrams, read the dictionary definitions of all the symbols, and apply quality tests to the work. The specific tests are based on the following criteria:

System models must be:

- *Complete* - All diagram symbols must be defined and all necessary non-symbol definitions, such as data elements, must exist.

- *Correct* - Each methodology contains rules, or diagram notation, for drawing diagrams. System Architect will examine the diagram and dictionary entries to verify adherence to the rules.

- *Consistent* - Consistency is measured in two dimensions:

    1. An individual diagram must be consistent within itself: For example, a data store definition must include all data elements that are specified on the combination of input and output data flows to that data store.

    2. A diagram must be consistent with other related diagrams in the model. For example, each "child diagram" must "balance" to its "parent symbol"; all the data entering a parent process and leaving it must also be represented on its attached child diagram.

10.3.1 Rule-Checking Programs

Rule-checking programs applicable to data modeling will be run in the following section. These programs include:

1. The *Rules Check* report which applies the rules of entity relation diagrams to the data model diagrams. For example, this report will examine the diagram to verify that all relation lines are connected to an entity on both ends.

2. The *Expression Check* report looks for defined expressions (elements and/or structures) for all symbols on the currently viewed diagram.

3. The *1st Normal Form Check* report searches the current diagram for expressions subject to normalization checks. For example, it looks for entities which may have been defined with a data field which has multiple occurrences for a single occurrence of the entity.

4. The *Second and Third Normal Forms Check* report searches the current diagram for expressions subject to normalization checks. For example, it looks for entities which may have been defined with duplicate data fields, thus resulting in data redundancy.

10.3.2 Running Rule-Checking Reports

Errors and inconsistencies can creep into the design during the months that a project team spends capturing the voluminous details of a new system. Specifically, errors concerning processing and data structures in the encyclopedia are introduced. System Architect provides a comprehensive set of rule-checking programs to assist in locating and eliminating problems. The rule-checking programs examine the diagrams, read the dictionary definitions of symbols contained in the diagram, and apply quality tests to the work. The tests check that the system models and definitions are complete, correct, and consistent.

Four rule-checking reports will be run using the ERD diagram created in *Chapter 8* and *Chapter 9*.

The more in-depth reports test for adherence to methodology-based rules, internal consistency within diagrams, and consistency with related diagrams. The rule-checking reports are in the REPORTS.RPT file. These reports can also be run from the methodology menu by selecting the report type from the **Entity-Rel** menu.

10.3.2.1 Rules Check Report

The *Rules Check* report is often the first rule-checking report to be run. This report checks for violations of entity relation diagram conventions. For example, all relation lines must be connected between two entities.

The *Rules Check* report is run from the methodology menu.

1. Open the *Library Database Diagram*.

2. Pull down the **Entity-Rel** menu and select the **Rules Check** command.

System Architect will check the current diagram for violations. If violations were found, it displays the results in a report such as the one in *Figure 10-4*. The report may be printed or viewed on-line, in order to assist you in correcting the violations.

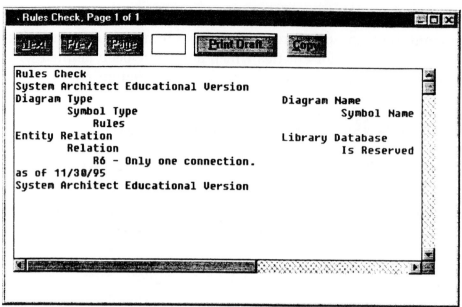

Figure 10-4. The Rules Check Report

If violations were discovered, System Architect also places error marks on the diagram where the violation occurred.

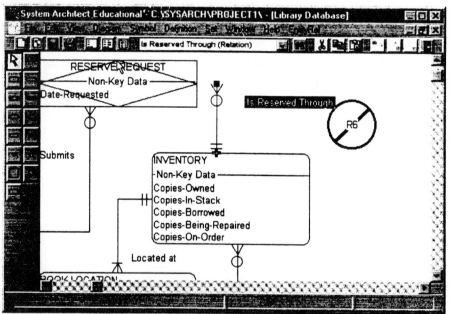

Figure 10-5. Error Markings

To remove the error markings from the diagram:

1. Pull down the **Entity-Rel** menu and select the **Clear Errors** command.

Once the error markings are removed, the diagram can be modified to correct the noted violations and the report can be re-run. If no violations are detected when the report is executed, a message window indicating the report is empty will be displayed.

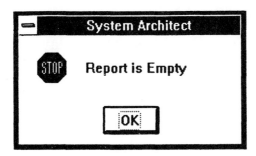

Figure 10-6. The **Report is Empty** Message

10.3.2.2 Expression Check Report

This report makes a complete data expression syntax check and validation, and updates all associated cross referencing. For example, the report checks for data elements or data structures which have not been properly defined.

To run the *Expression Check* report:

1. Pull down the **Entity-Rel** menu and select the **Expression Check** command.

2. Answer **No** to the "Save changes to diagram ---" dialog.

3. The *Expression Check report* is displayed.

4. Note any violations that need to be corrected.

10.3.2.3 Normalization Check Reports

The *First Normal Form Check* report and the *Second and Third Normal Forms Check* report searches the current diagram for expressions subject to normalization checks. For example, the first report looks for any repeating groups of data elements in an entity, and the second report looks for any data element that appears in more than one entity but is a key field in none.

To run the *1st Normal Form Check* report:

1. Pull down the **Entity-Rel** menu and select the **1ˢᵗ Normal Form Check** command.

2. Answer **No** to the "Save changes to diagram ---" dialog.

3. The *1st Normal Form Check report* is displayed.

4. Note any violations that need to be corrected.

To run the *2nd & 3rd Normal Form Check* report:

1. Pull down the **Entity-Rel** menu and select the **1ˢᵗ Normal Form Check** command.

2. Answer **No** to the "Save changes to diagram ---" dialog.

3. The *1ˢᵗ Normal Form Check report* is displayed.

4. Note any violations that need to be corrected.

Be sure to save your corrected diagram and then exit System Architect.

10.4 Questions in Review

1. What is the name of the file that System Architect defaults to, which contains over 100 pre-written reports?

2. Name the differences between printing a draft report and printing a fully formatted report.

3. What three criteria are rules checking reports based on?

4. Name four data modeling rule checking programs.

5. Which rule-checking report is usually the first to be run and checks for violations of entity relation diagram conventions?

6. Give an example of a violation in which running the Rules Check report would detect.

7. If when running a rule checking report violations are discovered, what happens to your diagram?

8. List the procedure to remove the error markings from a diagram.

9. When running a rules checking report, how does System Architect communicate that no violations were detected.

10. Give an example of a violation in which running the 2nd & 3rd Normal Forms Check report would detect.

Answers to the above questions can be found in Appendix B.

. Appendix A: Preference Options

Auto Associate is used to toggle on and off the automatic prompting of properties of line type symbols when they are added to a diagram. The specific dialog box presented varies depending on the line type symbol which is added. If **Auto Associate** is toggled off at the time the line is drawn, you can add associative properties at any time by selecting the line, pulling down the **Symbol** menu and clicking on the **Associative** command. A shortcut to the **Associative** dialog is to place the cursor on the line, click the right mouse button, and choose the **Associative** command from the pop-up menu.

Auto Define will prompt you for a dictionary definition as soon as the symbol was placed.

Auto Definition Delete will cause a definition entry to be deleted when a corresponding symbol is deleted from a diagram if the deleted symbol was the last occurrence of that symbol.

Auto Definition Rename will cause a dictionary entry to be renamed when the corresponding symbol is renamed if the renamed symbol was the last occurrence of that symbol.

Auto Name will prompt you to name the symbol as soon as it is placed on the diagram.

Auto Number will assign the next available number to a process symbol (or to other symbols as well if a style for that symbol has been set to allow auto numbering).

Auto Options will cause an options box to be displayed each time you place a symbol on a Character Screen, Graphic Screen, or Menu Screen.[1]

Auto Reposition Flag is used to toggle on and off the auto repositioning of flags attached to line type symbols. If **Auto Reposition Flag** is on, when the line type symbol is moved, or a rectangular symbol connected to the line type symbol is moved, the flag will be repositioned to the default position.

Auto Reposition Name will allow automatic repositioning of names connected to line type symbols.

---

[1] *Screen Painter* option.

Auto Horizontal Resize will allow rectangular symbols to be automatically expanded in the horizontal direction (i.e., width) to hold text. For example, when foreign keys are propagated on an Entity Relation or IDEF1X diagram, the initials (FK) are placed next to the attribute. Setting the Auto-Horizontal Resize preference to on will cause the width of the entity symbol to increase to compensate for the additional text.

Auto Vertical Resize will allow rectangular symbols to be automatically expanded vertically (i.e., height) to hold text. For example, if a graphic comment is added to an entity on an Entity Relation or IDEF1X diagram, the height of the entity will increase to compensate for the additional text if the Auto-Horizontal Resize preference is set to on.

Auto Propagate FK will automatically propagate foreign keys while relation lines are drawn. This function is triggered by a change in the Associative properties of the relation line. Therefore, the foreign keys will be automatically propagated when the cardinality of the line is defined. Foreign key elements will automatically be added to an entity in which a foreign key exists, changing the definition of the entity.

Auto Create FK Report will automatically produce a report of all modifications involved in the propagation of foreign keys. Note that this report cannot be duplicated after the foreign keys are established; therefore, if you want to refer back to it, you must first have the preference set to produce it, then propagate the foreign keys, then either print the report or copy it to a file.

Display Toolbox will automatically bring up the toolbox when you open a diagram.

Draw Truncation Indicator will place four circles in any symbol that has additional text that cannot be displayed within the symbol boundary.

Duplicate Check will warn you that your current choice of name for a specific symbol has already been used on the diagram.

Simultaneous/Select Draw will allow you to select symbols while in Draw mode. When this preference is selected, you must press and hold the mouse button for a count to draw a line. When this preference is not selected you must leave Draw mode, by either clicking on the cursor button in the toolbox or hitting the Esc key, before you attempt to select a symbol.

Immediate Auto-Routing will automatically re-route lines that were specified as having the **Automatic (Orthogonal)** line style (**Set** menu, **Line** command).

Verify Dialog will request a confirmation before changing levels to parent, child or other diagram.

Appendix B: Questions in Review Answers

B.1 Chapter 1

1. What is **System Architect**?

   System Architect is a PC-based CASE tool that maintains relationships between every object and every other object in a system, plus automates the process of generating, manipulating, organizing, and managing system-modeling diagrams.

2. Name five diagram types that System Architect supports.

   - *Gane & Sarson data flow*
   - *Ward & Mellor data flow (real time)*
   - *Yourdon/DeMarco data flow*
   - *Decomposition*
   - *Entity relation*
   - *Flow Chart*
   - *IDEF0*
   - *IDEF1X*
   - *Logical View*
   - *State transition*
   - *Ward & Mellor state transition*
   - *Structure chart*
   - *SSADM IV*
   - *Database Physical Models*
   - *Object-oriented design: Booch, Coad-Yourdon, & OMT (optional)*

- *Graphical User Interface (GUI) Screens and Menus (optional)*

- *Character-based Screens (optional)*

3. Define Systems modeling.

   Systems modeling is the process of describing an existing or proposed system. A model is constructed, which is used to analyze the system, and optimize its functionality.

4. What are graphic languages?

   Graphic languages are sets of symbols that, when used according to the rules of the methodology, can communicate the complex relationships of information systems more clearly than narrative text.

5. What does System Architect's encyclopedia consist of?

   The data dictionary together with the symbols, connections, and diagrams are referred to as the Encyclopedia.

B.2 Chapter 2

1. What is an **Audit ID**? What are its characteristics?

   An Audit ID is a personal identifier, but not a password. It can be any combination of letters and numbers up to seven characters.

2. What would be the name of the encyclopedia which resided in the directory C:\SYSARCH\PROJECT1? How many encyclopedias can be created in the Student Version of System Architect?

   "PROJECT1" would be the encyclopedia name.
   The Student Version allows up to two encyclopedias.

3. What menu and command would you use to modify your session's preference settings?

   To modify your preference settings, pull down the Set menu and click on the Preferences command.

4. How can a data domain be used?

   A data domain can be used to specify default physical properties to be shared by a group of data elements.

5. Define and compare Data Elements and Data Structures.

   A data element is the smallest unit of stored data, which means that it cannot be broken down further, or that it makes no sense to break it down further.

   Data Structures are convenient groupings of data (elements and/or other structures).

6. What is the syntax called for the following expression:
      "Data Expression A is composed of Component_B and Component_C and...".

   The syntax is called a sequence structure.

7. Why must data element and data structure names used in an expression adhere to stricter naming conventions than symbol names?

Data element and data structure names used in an expression must adhere to stricter naming conventions than symbol names because System Architect must distinguish the component as a unit and check for proper syntax.

8. System Architect supports over 100 different symbols types, but fewer definition types, why?

System Architect supports over 100 different symbols for the different diagrams and methodologies. But there are fewer definition types, because several different symbol types often map to a single definition type.

9. What is a System Architect comment?

A Comment is a free-form text field description that documents a single occurrence of a graphic symbol. Comments are limited to 4,095 characters.

10. What is a System Architect graphic comment?

The Graphic Comment also documents a single instance of a symbol, but it is limited to 1000 characters and can be displayed on a diagram.

B.3 Chapter 3

1. Define the process modeling technique.
Process modeling is a technique for describing the functional characteristics of a system. It involves the flow and transformation of data through the various processes of the system and the functional decomposition of these processes.

2. List three reasons for using the process-modeling approach.
Reasons for using the process-modeling approach include:

- *It provides a means for understanding complex systems.*
- *It provides a means for evaluating system requirements.*
- *It provides a simple and accurate language/method for communication between the clients, the users, and the development team.*
- *It provides a basis for the physical design.*
- *It creates a machine-readable repository of data that can evolve through later development stages and be used in the generation of the software.*

3. What is a context diagram and what does it consist of?
A context diagram is the top-most data flow diagram (DFD) in structured analysis. It usually consists of a single process symbol at the center of the page, surrounded by external entity symbols or "terminators" that feed data into the system and receive data from it.

4. What is the **DFD-GS** methodology menu?
It contains the symbol and line drawing commands you need to draw diagrams matching the Gane & Sarson data flow diagram standard, in addition to consistency and balancing reports.

5. Name three ways to toggle the Toolbox on and off for individual diagrams.

- *de-selecting **Toolbox** from the **View** menu*
- *de-selecting **Toolbox** from the floating diagram menu*
- *clicking the Toolbox icon on the Toolbar.*

6. When the cursor changes to a "pencil and rectangle", what does that indicate?
   The pencil indicates you are in "draw" mode, ready to place symbols in your diagram. The rectangle tells you that you will be placing a rectangular shaped symbol.

7. Which menu and command would you use to increase the number of grid points per inch?

   The View menu and the Grid & Reduced View command.

8. What two techniques can you use to save your diagram?
   - *Use the Save command from the Diagram menu.*
   - *Use the Save Diagram button on the toolbar.*

9. If you were to lose power to your PC, would all the work you have done, either creating or modifying a diagram, be lost since opening the diagram (or from your last save)?
   Yes.

10. List three ways to exit System Architect.
    - *Pull down the **File** menu, and click on the **Exit** command.*
    - *Double-click on the Control-menu box.*
    - *Single-click on the Control-menu box, then click on the Close command in the Control menu.*

B.4 Chapter 4

1. List the available line types and their characteristics offered with System Architect.

Line type	Characteristics
Straight, any orientation	Does not require bend points, but lines can be bent at any angle.
Straight orthogonal	To switch direction must have 1 or more bend points.
Automatic orthogonal	Exactly like straight orthogonal, but System Architect determines the bend points for you.
Elliptical arc	Curved line between rectangular symbols.

2. What is the Gane & Sarson diagram notation standard for data flow lines?
The Gane & Sarson diagram notation standard calls for all data flow line segments to be horizontal or vertical.

3. Assuming the line style is set to straight orthogonal, list two techniques to change the cursor to a "pencil and cross" in order to draw a data flow line.
Pull down the DFD-GS menu and select the Data Flow command or select the line symbol from the Toolbox.

4. What key would you press to stop drawing a line before you have attached it at both ends to a symbol?
If you want to stop drawing a line before you have attached it at both ends to a symbol, press the Escape key.

5. List the three ways a data flow arrowhead can be drawn and the meaning of each.
A line that is attached at both ends to symbols has a black arrowhead. A line that is attached at only one end to a symbol has a hatched arrowhead, that is, a partially filled-in arrowhead. A line that is not attached at either end to a symbol has a white arrowhead.

6. What is the difference between a data structure and a data element?
A data element is the smallest unit of data. A data structure is a grouping of related data elements.

7. What does the notation indicate when a data flow or material flow line is double-headed?
This notation indicates that the same data or material is exchanged in both directions between the external entity and the process.

8. What command could be used to place a descriptive title at the top of a data flow diagram?
The Text command.

9. What command could be used to place a rectangular symbol containing the diagram name and the creation/last modification date?
The Doc Block command.

10. What menu and command would you use to add a comment to a Doc Block?
Use the Symbol menu and Name, Number, Properties command.

B.5 Chapter 5

1. When in "Select Mode", what shape is the cursor in order to move a symbol?
   The cursor is an arrow shape.

2. List two methods to "de-select" a symbol.
   To "de-select" a symbol, either select any other symbol, or move the cursor anywhere outside of a symbol to white space and click the left mouse button.

3. List the procedure for removing bends from a data flow line.
   - *Select the data flow line by simultaneously pointing to the line and clicking the right mouse button, resulting in the line being selected and the Line pop-menu appearing.*
   - *Select the **Reduce Line Segment** command. All bends will now be removed from the line.*

4. What shape will the cursor change to when selecting the **Insert Line Segment** command?
   The cursor will change to a "pencil and line with 3 handles" shape.

5. If a data flow name has been properly positioned, what must you do to prevent the name from being moved by System Architect when the data flow line is repositioned.
   To prevent data flow names from being moved by System Architect once they have been properly positioned, toggle the Auto Reposition Name option to OFF.

6. List the three methods for removing an unwanted symbol.
   Method 1. Press the "Delete Last Symbol key", F9.
   Pressing the F9 key deletes the last placed symbol on a diagram.

   Method 2. Select the unwanted symbol and press the Delete key.

   *Method 3. Select the unwanted symbol, pull down the **Edit** menu and select the **Delete** command.*

7. What function does the F10 key serve?
   The F10 key will select symbols in the order in which they were placed on the diagram.

8. What must you do to ensure the symbols in your data flow diagrams are numbered consecutively?
To make sure the symbols in your data flows are numbered consecutively, Auto Number must be toggled on in the Preferences Dialog.

9. List the three types of pop-up menus available in System Architect.
Three types of pop-up menus are available in System Architect: one for diagram commands, one for rectangular symbol commands, and one for line symbol commands.

10. Under what condition will the commands **Child Create** and **Child Attach** be included in the pop-up menu for a symbol?
The Child Create and Child Attach commands will only be included in the pop-up menu for a symbol that has not yet been expanded to a child diagram.

B.6 Chapter 6

1. Define "leveling".
   "Leveling" can be defined through the following four statements:
   - *The diagram contains a given process symbol, the parent process, in which the complexity of the process is hidden.*
   - *The parent process symbol is expanded into an entire child diagram that is used to explain the hidden complexity of the process.*
   - *Therefore, the parent process and the child diagram are equivalent.*
   - *This is a logical equivalence; therefore, any data flowing into the parent process symbol must also flow into the child diagram. Similarly, any data flowing out of the parent process symbol must also flow out of the child diagram.*

2. How would System Architect number three processes in a child diagram, if the process in the parent diagram was numbered P1?
   P1.1, P1.2, AND P1.3

3. In the **Child Create** dialog, the **Name** field is already filled in with the name of the parent process. Why is this a good standard to follow?
   This standard is considered to be a good one to follow - since the child diagram and the parent process are one and the same, only the level of detail has changed.

4. When creating a child diagram, System Architect presents you with a dialog box containing three choices of material to placed on the child diagram. What are the three choices of material?
   Image of Parent Symbol, Lines/Flows Attached to Parent, and Symbols Attached to Lines/Flows.

5. What is an "uncle" symbol?
   Those are the symbols at the opposite end of the flow lines attached to the parent symbol.

6. Does System Architect support the use of multiple windows? Why would you use multiple windows?
   Yes. To be able to view the child and the parent diagrams on the same screen.

7. What is the fill pattern of the arrowhead of a data flow line that is properly attached to symbols at both ends?
Solid.

8. To place duplicate symbols in a diagram what option must be turned off?
To duplicate a symbol, the option Duplicate Check must be turned off in the preferences dialog.

9. List the procedure for converting a one-line data flow name into a two-line data flow name?
To place a two-line data flow name:
   - *Select the name to be changed.*
   - *Pull down the Symbol menu and click Name, Number, Properties.*
   - *Click in the + button to expand the Name field.*
   - *Enter a carriage return where you would like to end the first line.*
   - *Type the remainder of the name onto the next line in the dialog box.*

10. When creating a multi-line data flow name, why must you place a blank character at the end of the line before the carriage return?
A blank character must be placed at the end of each line before the carriage return. Otherwise, System Architect will not register the blank characters in the process names; i.e., it will read Check Out Books as CheckOutBooks. There may be level balancing problems later.

B.7 Chapter 7

1. What is the name of the file that System Architect defaults to, which contains over 100 pre-written reports?
REPORTS.RPT

2. Name the differences between printing a draft report and printing a fully formatted report.
A draft report can be composed much quicker than a fully-formatted printout. Font commands, such as bold or italic are ignored when creating a draft report. Format commands, such as width, and graphics commands, such as underline or draw borders, are also ignored.

3. What three criteria are rules checking reports based on?
The specific tests are based on the following criteria:

   System models must be:
   - *Complete - All diagram symbols must be defined and all necessary non-symbol definitions, such as data elements, must exist.*
   - *Correct - Each methodology contains rules, or diagram notation, for drawing diagrams. System Architect will examine the diagram and dictionary entries to verify adherence to the rules. For example, each process on data flow diagrams must have at least one input data flow and one output data flow.*
   - *Consistent - Consistency is measured in two dimensions:*
     - *An individual diagram must be consistent within itself: For example, a data store definition must include all data elements that are specified on the combination of input and output data flows to that data store.*
     - *A diagram must be consistent with other related diagrams in the model. For example, each "child diagram" must "balance" to its "parent symbol"; all the data entering a parent process and leaving it must also be represented on its attached child diagram.*

4. Name four process modeling rule checking programs.
   - **The Rules Check**
   - **The Balance Children**
   - **The Balance Parent**
   - **The Balance Horizontal**
   - **The Expression Check**

5. Which rule-checking report is usually the first to be run and checks for violations of data flow diagram conventions?
   Rules Check Report

6. What is it called if a process does not have at least one input data flow and one output data flow?
   Black Hole or Miracle

7. If when running a rule checking report violations are discovered, what happens to your diagram?
   If violations were discovered, System Architect places error marks on the diagram where the violation occurred.

8. What is the procedure to remove the error markings from a diagram.
   To remove the error markings from the diagram:
   - **Pull down the DFD-GS menu and select the Clear Errors command**

9. Define the *Balance Children* report.
   The Balance Child(ren) report checks that one diagram is consistent with another related diagram in the model. For example, each child diagram must balance to its parent symbol. That is, all the data elements entering a parent process and leaving it, must also be represented on its attached child diagram. If not, the parent symbol and child diagram do not represent the same input-process/output activity.

10. List the procedure for running the *Balance Parent* report.
   To run the Balance Parent report:
   - **Open the child diagram.**
   - **Pull down the DFD-GS menu and select the Balance Parent command.**
   - **Answer No to the "Save changes to diagram —" dialog.**
   - **The Balance Parent report is displayed.**

B.8 Chapter 8

1. Define a weak entity.
    A weak, or dependent entity depends on another entity for its existence. At least one of the primary keys will always be a foreign key.

2. Define an access path.
    The access path, sometimes referred to as an alternate index, represents an alternate way to read a given row from a table. The access path may, or may not, be a unique identifier.

3. List two ways the Symbol Locate list box can be used.
    The Symbol Locate list box can be used in two ways. If a symbol is selected, its name and type is displayed in the box. On the other hand, if you want to rapidly locate any symbol on a diagram, find its name in the list and select it. Then click on the binoculars. The focus of the diagram immediately shifts to the chosen symbol.

4. True or False: There is a unique toolbox for every methodology menu.
    True.

5. List three ways to toggle the Toolbox on or off.
    You can toggle the Toolbox on and off for individual diagrams by:

    - *de-selecting Toolbox from the View menu*
    - *de-selecting Toolbox from the pop-up diagram menu*
    - *clicking the Toolbox icon on the Toolbar*

6. What is System Architect's default value for reduced view?
    The System Architect default value for reduced view is 75%.

7. List two techniques to change the cursor to a "pencil and rectangle" in order to draw an entity symbol.
    - *Pull down the EntityRel menu and select Entity*
    - *Select the Entity symbol from the Toolbox*

8. When defining an entity, what does the @ sign indicate?
    The @ sign indicates the attribute is the primary key, or part of a composite(or concatenated) primary key.

9. True or False: System Architect automatically saves changes to a diagram as soon as they occur.
    False. For changes to a diagram to be saved, System Architect must be instructed to save the diagram.

10. List three ways to exit System Architect.
    There are three ways to exit System Architect:

    - *Pull down the File menu, and click on the Exit command.*

    - *Double-click on the Control-menu box.*

    - *Single-click on the Control-menu box, then click on the Close command in the Control menu.*

B.9 Chapter 9

1. What is a sub-entity?
   Sub-entities represent categorizations of the super-entity type.

2. Define an associative entity.
   An associative entity is a weak entity that exists for the sole purpose of resolving a many-to-many relationship. All of the primary keys of an associative entity are foreign keys, inherited from the entities for which the many-to-many relationship is resolved.

3. List the available line types and their characteristics offered with System Architect.

Line type	Characteristics
Straight, any orientation	*Does not require bend points, but lines can be bent at any angle.*
Straight orthogonal	*To switch direction must have 1 or more bend points.*
Automatic orthogonal	*Exactly like straight orthogonal, but System Architect determines the bend points for you.*
Elliptical arc	*Curved line between rectangular symbols.*

4. Which two line types are appropriate to use for data models?
   - *Straight orthogonal*
   - *Automatic (orthogonal)*

5. List the two methods to enter "drawing mode" in order to draw relation lines.
   - *Pull down the EntityRel menu and select the Relation command.*
   - *Select the relation line from the Toolbox.*

6. Why must relation lines always be started at the source entity and end at the target entity?
   Relation lines on Entity Relation diagrams should always be started at the source entity and ended at the target entity because the source/target designation cannot be changed.

7. What key would you press to stop drawing a line before it is attached and return to "select mode."
   Escape key.

8. The cardinality of a relation line is specified using which dialog box?

The Associative Properties dialog box.

9. When System Architect draws a dotted line which encompasses two more entities, what does that signify?
It indicates that a super/sub entity relationship exists among the entities within the dotted line.

10. What does the **Display Mode** command allow you to do?
The Display Mode command allows the user to display definition information directly on the diagram.

B.10 Chapter 10

1. What is the name of the file that System Architect defaults to, which contains over 100 pre-written reports?
REPORTS.RPT

2. Name the differences between printing a draft report and printing a fully formatted report.
A draft report can be composed much quicker than a fully-formatted printout. Font commands, such as bold or italic are ignored when creating a draft report. Format commands, such as width, and graphics commands, such as underline or draw borders, are also ignored.

3. What three criteria are rules checking reports based on?
The specific tests are based on the following criteria:

System models must be:
- *Complete - All diagram symbols must be defined and all necessary non-symbol definitions, such as data elements, must exist.*
- *Correct - Each methodology contains rules, or diagram notation, for drawing diagrams. System Architect will examine the diagram and dictionary entries to verify adherence to the rules. For example, each process on data flow diagrams must have at least one input data flow and one output data flow.*
- *Consistent - Consistency is measured in two dimensions:*
  - *An individual diagram must be consistent within itself: For example, a data store definition must include all data elements that are specified on the combination of input and output data flows to that data store.*
  - *A diagram must be consistent with other related diagrams in the model. For example, each "child diagram" must "balance" to its "parent symbol"; all the data entering a parent process and leaving it must also be represented on its attached child diagram.*

4. Name four data modeling rule checking programs.
    - *The Rules Check*
    - *The Expression Check*
    - *The 1st Normal Form Check*
    - *The 2nd & 3rd Normal Forms Check*

5. Which rule-checking report is usually the first to be run and checks for violations of entity relation diagram conventions?
    Rules Check Report

6. Give an example of a violation in which running the Rules Check report would detect.
    A relation line is not connected to an entity on both ends.

7. If when running a rule checking report violations are discovered, what happens to your diagram?
    If violations were discovered, System Architect places error marks on the diagram where the violation occurred.

8. List the procedure to remove the error markings from a diagram?
    To remove the error markings from the diagram:
    - *Pull down the Entity-Rel menu and select the Clear Errors command.*

9. When running a rules checking report, how does System Architect communicate that no violations were detected.
    If no violations are detected when the report is executed, a message window indicating the report is empty will be displayed.

10. Give an example of a violation in which running the 2nd & 3rd Normal Forms Check report would detect.
    A data element appears in more than one entity but is a key field in none.

. Appendix C: System Architect Educational Versions

The educational version of System Architect consists of three modes of operation and are detailed below.

C.1 The Student Version (Book Mode) As Shipped

When operating in "Book Mode" (as shipped) you can create 2 project encyclopedias. In each encyclopedia you can:

- Create 10 diagrams of any type

- Place a total of 300 symbols (combined total for all diagrams)

- Create a total of 400 definitions (including definitions for diagram objects and data)

C.2 The Lab Mode Version

The "Lab Mode" version which uses the University version of SAEDUCA.DLL enhances the "Book Mode" by increasing the number of diagrams and definitions which can be created, and the number of symbols which can be placed on diagrams. In each of your 2 encyclopedias you can:

- Create 30 diagrams of any type

- Place a total of 900 symbols (combined total for all diagrams)

- Create a total of 1200 definitions (including definitions for diagram objects and data)

- Access any size model created in the University version of System Architect.

  If the encyclopedia is within the size restrictions specified above, you will have read/write access. If it exceeds the size limitations, you will be able to view it in read only mode.

C.3 The University Version

The University version of System Architect has all of the functionality of the commercial version of the product. There are no restrictions on the number, or size, of encyclopedias that may be created. The University version is designed for use in your school's computer laboratory only.

Do not copy the software from your school's network installation. Copying the university's software to any other computer is an infringement of the copyright laws. In addition, the University version of System Architect requires a copy protection device.